MEXICO
Under Fox

A PUBLICATION OF

The Americas SOCIETY — AND —   CIDAC

MEXICO
Under Fox

edited by
Luis Rubio
Susan Kaufman Purcell

LYNNE
RIENNER
PUBLISHERS

BOULDER
LONDON

Published in the United States of America in 2004 by
Lynne Rienner Publishers, Inc.
1800 30th Street, Boulder, Colorado 80301
www.rienner.com

and in the United Kingdom by
Lynne Rienner Publishers, Inc.
3 Henrietta Street, Covent Garden, London WC2E 8LU

Library of Congress Cataloging-in-Publication Data
Mexico under Fox / edited by Luis Rubio & Susan Kaufman Purcell.
"A publication of the Americas Society."
Includes bibliographical references and index.
ISBN 1-58826-242-1 (hc : alk. paper)
ISBN 1-58826-218-9 (pb : alk. paper)
  1. Mexico—Politics and government—1988– . 2. Mexico—Economic conditions.
3. Mexico—Social conditions. 4. Mexico—Foreign relations—United States.
5. United States—Foreign relations—Mexico. I. Rubio-Freidberg, Luis.
II. Purcell, Susan Kaufman.
F1236.M483 2004
972.08'35—dc22   2003023331

British Cataloguing in Publication Data
A Cataloguing in Publication record for this book
is available from the British Library.

Printed and bound in the United States of America

 The paper used in this publication meets the requirements
of the American National Standard for Permanence of
Paper for Printed Library Materials Z39.48-1992.

5 4 3 2 1

Contents

Illustrations

Foreword

Few people fully appreciate the enormity of the changes that have taken place in Mexico in recent years. In the space of less than two decades, the country liberalized its economy, organized fair and respected electoral processes, lived through a period of divided government, and in 2000 experienced the defeat of the Institutional Revolutionary Party (PRI) for the presidency. Given the PRI's seventy-year-long tenure as the ruling party, as well as its influence over everything from education to economic production, land distribution, and foreign affairs, the impact of this defeat cannot be overstated.

Mexicans now live in a climate of political freedom, a remarkable development after almost a century of authoritarian rule. The media are increasingly independent, and some progress is being made in combating corruption. Civil society is becoming more vibrant, with young people more prone to engage in politics and growing activism by nongovernmental organizations. Foreign policy, too, has come to reflect Mexico's more open political climate through a greater emphasis on supporting human rights and democracy.

Yet, challenges remain. While political freedom is undoubtedly welcome, many Mexicans have yet to experience any tangible benefits from the political and economic transformations that have taken place. When Vicente Fox of the National Action Party (PAN) assumed the presidency in December 2000, expectations of such benefits were heightened even further. To understand why these expectations remain largely unmet, it is helpful to recognize that the changes Mexico has undergone were neither planned nor anticipated. Both electoral reform and economic liberalization can best be understood as reactions to events, domestic and foreign, rather than as visionary transformations. The inevitable result is that change has been piecemeal and incremental, and the institutions of Mexican society have not fully adapted to the new realities of power. The legislative branch is a case in point: its structure and governance remain virtually unaltered from the years of PRI rule, when the president's views were dominant. Nevertheless, Mexicans are living in an era in which the presidency has become uncoupled from the leadership of the PRI, and the office no longer enjoys the power it once did. Congress has become a check on presidential powers, but without many of the balances necessary to make the system work.

On the economic front, the reforms of the early 1990s were supposed to be the first stage of a major transformation that would strengthen the domestic economy, integrate it with the rest of the world, and improve the lot of the average Mexican. The signing of the North American Free Trade Agreement (NAFTA) with the United States and Canada in 1993 was seen as a guarantee that there would be no backtracking by Mexico regarding those reforms. However, once the reforms were put in place and NAFTA came into being, efforts stopped short of adjusting legislation, modernizing institutions, and enabling domestic producers to compete. As long as the U.S. economy made it possible for Mexican exports to grow at a double-digit annual pace, nobody paid much attention to the lack of further reforms and the incomplete process of adjustment. However, once the U.S. economy ceased to grow, Mexicans were confronted with an unpleasant fact: little had been done to shield Mexico from the effects of recession in the north or to find new engines for domestic growth.

In contrast to the early 1990s when most reforms were launched, the current political environment makes it difficult to complete the process of transition. A relatively weak presidency and a disorganized Congress mean that agreements can be reached only if they do not entail costs for any of society's powerful interests. In fact, as in many democracies, special interests have found in this new political environment endless opportunity to try to roll back some of the previous reforms, advance their particular interests, and paralyze the reform process.

If one takes a broader view of Mexican history, it is clear that this turn of events is not unique. Mexico has generally advanced at an incremental pace, taking two steps forward and one step backward, rather than through decisive strides. Successive administrations have introduced reform measures only to see them partially reversed by subsequent governments. While progress is made, it is less dramatic than it might be otherwise.

With the Fox administration now in the second half of its six-year tenure, it is an ideal moment to assess how much progress has indeed been made. *Mexico Under Fox* brings together an array of authors who are not only astute analysts of Mexican politics and economics, but also practitioners and policymakers with firsthand experience of the issues they are addressing. Mexico is a country whose importance to the United States and its citizens continues to grow. We hope that the authors' insights into the relationship between economic and political liberalization, the unfinished agenda of reform, and the impact of both on U.S.-Mexican relations, will contribute to a fuller understanding of Mexico's future and the future of the bilateral relationship.

—*Edna Jaime*
General Director, CIDAC

—*Susan Segal*
President, Americas Society

Acknowledgments

This book is the product of the combined efforts of a number of people and organizations. We held two authors' group sessions to discuss the first draft of the manuscript, one in Mexico City at the Centro de Investigación para el Desarrollo, A.C. (CIDAC), and one in New York at the Americas Society. Thanks to Stephen Blank, Douglas Chalmers, Robert Kaufman, Javier Murcio, Roberto Newell, Gray Newman, and Alfredo Thorne for their very helpful comments at these meetings.

We especially appreciate the help of Jeffrey Gontero, assistant to the vice president of the Americas Society, for his extensive efforts in preparing the manuscript. We thank Rachel Gottesfeld, former assistant to the vice president, for her work in organizing the New York authors' group meeting. Thanks also to Susan Davis, senior director of programs at the Americas Society, and Pablo Iragorri, program officer in the office of the vice president, for helping with the financial aspects of the project. We also benefited from the research of two Americas Society interns, Eric Sigmon and Juliana Vajda, and from the editorial comments of Deirdre McCormack.

Our two editors, Judith Evans and Michelle Miller-Adams, did an excellent job in clarifying ideas and unifying the style of the various chapters. It was a pleasure to work with both of them. Thanks also to Susan Stephen for her admirable translations into English of the chapters originally written in Spanish. We are also grateful to the staff at Lynne Rienner Publishers for their important contributions to the editorial and publication processes.

This book and the authors' review groups associated with it were made possible by a generous grant from the Tinker Foundation Inc. to CIDAC for a collaborative project with the Americas Society. We particularly value the continued support of its chairman, Martha Muse, and its president, Renate Rennie, for our two institutions.

—Luis Rubio
—Susan Kaufman Purcell

MEXICO
Under Fox

Mexico

The States of Mexico

Introduction

Luis Rubio & Susan Kaufman Purcell

On December 1, 2000, Vicente Fox was inaugurated as president of Mexico. He brought with him promises of change and affirmation that Mexico had finally joined the ranks of democratic nations. The election of Fox—the successful candidate of the National Action Party (PAN)—the previous July had marked the first time that the long-ruling Institutional Revolutionary Party (PRI) had failed to secure the presidency. It also marked the culmination of a process of political and economic reform that had been building for fifteen years.

Since the mid-1980s, successive PRI administrations had sought to open Mexico's economy to international competition, reducing the role of the state and tying the nation's fortunes to its more affluent neighbors, the United States and Canada, through the North American Free Trade Agreement (NAFTA). Shortly thereafter a process of gradual political change began that resulted in opposition-party gains in state and local elections, then the loss of the PRI majority in Congress in 1997, and finally the defeat of the PRI candidate for the presidency and the election of Fox.

Yet neither the economic nor the political reform process is complete. While the degree and speed of change in Mexico's economy and society are remarkable, many difficult actions remain to be taken. Fox came to power vowing further change, but to many the achievements of his administration have fallen short. The purpose of this volume is to assess both the accomplishments and the shortcomings of the Fox administration to date and point the way toward the measures that must be taken if Mexico is to achieve greater political, economic, and social development. The authors bring to this task not only a scholarly understanding of the issues at hand, but also practical knowledge born of their extensive experience in the policy sphere.

The book builds on a series of papers first commissioned for a collaborative book project between the Centro de Investigación para el Desarrollo, A.C. (CIDAC), in Mexico City and the Americas Society in New York City that began in 2002. The papers were revised during 2003, partly to take into account the results of the July midterm elections in Mexico that dealt a setback to the president's party. Although the first drafts of the chapters were discussed during two authors' review meetings in both Mexico City and New York City with outside experts, the published book reflects the personal views of the individual authors.

In the first chapter, Luis Rubio traces the evolution of Mexico's political system, uncovering the roots of both economic and political reform. He makes clear the connection between the two, showing in the process what made Fox's victory possible. The chapter also addresses some of the complexities of Mexico's new democratic politics. These include the lack of institutions to accommodate the new political reality and an executive-legislative standoff that has created gridlock in the nation's politics. Finally, the author raises troubling concerns about what he calls the "noninstitutional side of Mexican politics"—those informal institutions that are willing to pursue their interests through illegal and sometimes violent means. He argues that these actors—and, more important, their ties to elements within Mexico's political parties—threaten to undermine Mexican democracy and the stability of the nation.

In Chapter 2, Edna Jaime focuses attention on the history of Mexico's economic reform process, set in motion twenty years ago, arguing that it has ground to a halt. She offers important insights into the link between politics and economics, showing, for example, why almost every *sexenio* (six-year presidential term) has culminated in a currency crisis, as governments increase public spending and maintain an overvalued peso in the run-up to elections. The chapter addresses not only key industrial sectors, such as electricity and energy, but also the problems plaguing the rural sector and why they have been so difficult to resolve. Throughout, Jaime underscores the central paradox of Mexico's economic reform process: that, while the economy overall has been opened to international competition, strategic sectors remain protected because of the strength of vested interests. She credits the Fox administration with maintaining macroeconomic stability, but finds disappointing its inability to reinvigorate or complete the unfinished economic reform process.

Chapter 3, by Juan Pardinas, focuses on Mexico's social problems, including high poverty rates, low educational quality, and shortcomings in the healthcare system. The policy response of the Fox government to date in these areas is assessed, with particular attention given to the problem of scarce resources. The author notes that the most remarkable—and positive—aspect of President Fox's antipoverty program is that it represents a marked continuity with the policies of his predecessor that were targeted toward the poor and linked to improvements in human capital. Another hopeful development has been greater transparency in the process of measuring poverty. But the chapter identifies important aspects of social policy that remain wanting, including the continued role of vested interests and barriers to reform, especially in the area of education, and subsidies that claim to help the poor but that actually direct their benefits elsewhere. Finally, the author offers a blueprint of what needs to be done in the social sphere, not just by the Fox administration in its final years but also by future governments.

The second half of the volume offers three perspectives on U.S.-Mexican relations—an appropriate emphasis given the importance of the United States to the Mexican economy and foreign policy. In Chapter 4, Andrés Rozental provides an analysis of the Fox government's overall international agenda. He introduces the key foreign policy priorities laid out by the administration at the beginning of its term, among them a new emphasis on the promotion of democracy and human rights, protection of the rights of Mexicans living abroad, the more prominent role Mexico has played in the multilateral sphere (through, for example, its seat on the United Nations Security Council), and, above all, the effort to recast the North American relationship through a comprehensive migration agreement with the United States. The author finds that this ambitious agenda has had mixed results: while the day-to-day aspects of foreign policy and especially relations with the United States are being handled smoothly, there is a growing sense of frustration among Mexicans over the failure to achieve progress on a migration accord and over the sense that the United States is neglecting its relationship with Mexico in light of foreign policy priorities elsewhere.

Chapter 5, by Luis Carlos Ugalde, focuses on the impact of democratization in Mexico on the bilateral relationship with the United States. He tackles the question of why the Fox administration's attempt to craft a migration agreement with the United States failed, and whether it might have been handled differently. The chapter takes issue with the argument that it was largely the events of September 11, 2001, that derailed progress on a migration accord, pointing to deeper factors that made such a comprehensive agreement unlikely. More broadly, the author finds that democratization has had contradictory effects on the ability of the executive to formulate foreign policy: while it has opened the way for Mexico to play a greater role on the international stage, it has also brought about new constraints on the executive's ability to make foreign policy, such as an increasingly active Congress and the role of public opinion.

In the final chapter, Susan Kaufman Purcell offers an overview of the bilateral relationship both before and after 2000. She identifies growing economic ties in the 1990s, especially the creation of NAFTA, as a fundamental factor in paving the way for warmer relations between the two nations. The 2000 presidential elections brought the United States and Mexico even closer together—in part because of the personal relationship between Presidents Bush and Fox—but serious conflicts remain. These include disagreements over the extent to which NAFTA should be "deepened" (especially in the area of migration), hemispheric security, the reaction to the events of September 11, and the U.S.-led war in Iraq. The author concludes by noting that the benign economic and international environment that facilitated greater cooperation in the 1990s is no longer in place, making it increasingly difficult to achieve the kind of "win-win" situation that characterized U.S.-Mexican relations until 2001. Nonetheless, she stresses that the interests of the two nations are so closely linked in the areas of the economy, immigration, and control of the drug trade that, even if Mexico has become a lower priority on the U.S. foreign policy agenda, it will not remain so for long.

1

Democratic Politics in Mexico: New Complexities

Luis Rubio

On July 2, 2000, Mexico entered a new era. After seven decades of one-party rule, Mexicans voted to oust the Institutional Revolutionary Party (PRI) from power, thereby launching the nation into the realm of democratic politics. While the impact of the PRI's defeat must not be underestimated, average Mexicans have yet to see any direct benefits from their newfound democracy. Instead, they are finding that decisions are slower under democratic rule and that the expectation of sudden improvements in daily life has been largely unmet.

Elections are a critical component of democratic politics; however, they are far from sufficient. A country may conduct an impeccable electoral process, as Mexico did in 2000, and yet produce a dysfunctional system of government. Having elected a president from a political party other than the PRI for the first time in modern history, Mexicans expected rapid changes in the country's politics and increased economic benefits. Well into the presidential term of Vicente Fox, Mexicans are coming to realize that more than the electoral process will need to be changed in order for democracy to deliver on its promises.

Mexico's democracy is still incomplete. On the one hand, power has shifted from one party to another as a result of an election, underscoring the fact that the nation has begun to develop institutions and mechanisms capable of settling disputes in a nonviolent way. This creates the possibility of further political change within a framework of stability, something no Mexican could have taken for granted only a few years ago. On the other hand, two features of the political landscape pose continuing challenges to the development of Mexican democracy. First, the removal of the presidency from control of the PRI has revealed constitutionally based weaknesses in Mexico's political structure and brought about an executive-legislative standoff that has created

5

gridlock in the nation's politics. And while new institutional rules are desperately needed, nobody has the incentives to exercise the leadership or forge the compromises necessary to create them.

Second, while the nation's formal political institutions (the presidency, Congress, political parties, and many interest groups) have begun the complex process of adjusting to competitive politics, there is a noninstitutional side of Mexican politics that has not. This set of largely informal institutions, which has been developing over the past several decades, includes groups representing land invaders, militant unions who hold a monopoly in their sectors, illegal taxi drivers, and other participants in the unofficial economy. These groups, which are willing to pursue their interests through illegal and sometimes violent means, threaten to undermine Mexican democracy and the stability of the nation as a whole. Their actions are all the more difficult to curtail because vested interests within the PRI and the left-wing Party of the Democratic Revolution (PRD) often intermingle with those of the noninstitutional players, sometimes making it impossible to differentiate between the two. The key question facing Mexico today is whether it will be able to bring these noninstitutional actors into the formal political arena and create the institutions necessary for its new democracy to function.

Where Is Mexico Coming From?

The elections of 2000 were the culmination of a process of internal transformation that began in the mid-1980s and marked the beginning of a period of adjustment that is still under way. In this sense, the new democratic Mexico is a work in progress. The history of Mexico's modern political system began in the late 1920s when the winners of the Mexican Revolution (1910–1917) came together to try to introduce a sense of order into the disarray and devastation that a long and bloody civil war had produced. After a decade of gradual political development, the country had stabilized, but it had not produced an institutional framework that could bring economic prosperity. While the victors had succeeded in agreeing on the text of the 1917 Constitution, there was no set of institutions available to organize the nation's various political groupings and clusters. The constitution had been the result of compromise among the various interests, most of which succeeded in getting their political interests and ideological perspectives represented in one or another article of the document. The process thus failed to produce a coherent framework that could serve as a foundation for development.

Hence, in recognition of these realities, in 1928, President Plutarco Elias Calles called for the creation of a political party that would incorporate all the leaders of factions, political parties, unions, militias, and other interests into a single organization. The new entity, called the National Revolutionary Party (PNR), would provide stability and reduce political violence. Eventually, the party would organize the groups led by its members into four distinct sectors: labor, peasants, popular organizations, and the military (later disbanded once it became a professional force).

The PNR was created with the dual purpose of controlling various political forces and institutionalizing the political system. The "carrot" provided to political groupings was the promise of access to power and wealth in exchange for loyalty to the system in general and the president in particular. Overriding allegiance to the president was balanced by the proviso that no president could remain in office for longer than a single six-year presidential term, or *sexenio*. This arrangement lasted from the 1920s until the late 1990s.

The PNR, later renamed the Party of the Mexican Revolution (PRM) and then the Institutional Revolutionary Party, evolved into a full-fledged electoral machine and system of control, complete with pork barrel spending and mechanisms to allocate benefits. Though created to control and channel power, the postrevolutionary political system served the country well. After years of infighting and violence at the beginning of the century, PRI rule brought about decades of political stability and economic growth. In the 1950s and 1960s, growth averaged above 7 percent a year, accompanied by low levels of inflation. The system was underpinned not just by loyalty, but also by corruption. All political actors were required to follow the lead of the party and the president, while understanding that they would be compensated for their cooperation. Compensation came in the form of access to power and positions that made it possible for individuals to become wealthy (both elected office and political appointment were effectively within presidential control). Discipline and corruption went hand in hand. Discipline stemmed from the promise that all those who behaved would be compensated. In turn, those who played by the so-called unwritten rules of the game (i.e., loyalty to the president and the system) usually found themselves with opportunities to exploit appointed positions for personal gain, never having to fear that they might be prosecuted. Members of the PRI used to say that the issue was not whether the glass was half full or half empty, but to be inside the glass. Accountability was to the president and the system, and success was reflected in terms of economic growth. Elections were critical not because they allowed for the

alternation of parties in government, but because they conferred legitimacy upon the system. The system was built on the premise that all who
behaved would benefit, thus making it unnecessary to exert force or
repression to guarantee stability. However, all governments from the
1920s through the late 1960s were as willing to exercise force as they
were to buy loyalty in order to maintain their power and credibility.

But the country was changing. At the turn of the twentieth century,
most Mexicans had lived in rural areas; by the late 1960s most of them
were city dwellers. A middle class had emerged and the business community was thriving. These demographic changes brought about a new
economic, social, and political climate. Nineteen sixty-eight ushered in
a period of radical change. That summer, a series of demonstrations
organized by university students led to clashes with the police and army
and to the deaths of at least thirty students in the Plaza de Tlatelolco,
in the center of Mexico City. Students were disgruntled about the structure of university governance and about the nation's politics, but they
were also joining students in other nations, mainly France, in a year of
worldwide protests. Though the actual events were short-lived, their
political impact could hardly have been greater. Many politicians inter-
preted the student movement as a signal of discontent with the political
system and evidence of the PRI's inability to accommodate a population
that had grown and become more diverse over the years.

In 1970, a new administration took office, and under Luis Echeverría's leadership (1970–1976) began making fundamental changes in the
economy. Abandoning decades of fiscal prudence, the government
embraced populism and nationalism and began priming the economy
with rapidly growing government expenditures financed by foreign debt
and inflation. Companies were expropriated and many new government
firms, offices, and regulations came into being. José López Portillo
(1976–1982) followed suit, pursuing similar inflationary policies, and
by 1982 the government was confronted with the need to default on its
huge foreign debt. Thus began a pattern of economic crises that seemed
to occur every six years.

During the 1980s, the government's main challenge was to deal
with the economic consequences of default. It took several years to
acknowledge that a new economic foundation for growth was needed,
but in 1985 the government liberalized imports and initiated other measures to open the economy to international competition. Some minor government concerns were privatized and others were shut down, while
many regulations were eliminated. However, these actions failed to
revitalize the economy and, by 1988, when Miguel de la Madrid's term
(1982–1988) ended, an important contingent of the left of the PRI

departed from the party, largely in protest over the economic reforms, and launched the candidacy of Cuauhtémoc Cárdenas for the presidency. Cárdenas, the son of the revered president of the 1930s who had expropriated the foreign oil companies, claimed his father's mantle and called for the adoption of nationalistic policies and the abandonment of the reforms that had recently been enacted. His group rejected any closeness with the United States and called for policies to support domestic producers. In the wake of Cárdenas's defeat in the 1988 elections, which he claimed to have won, those factions that had broken away from the PRI joined with several leftist political parties, such as the Communist Party, the Unified Mexican Socialist Party, and the Workers Revolutionary Party, to form the PRD, bringing Mexico's third major political party into being.

When Carlos Salinas took office at the end of 1988, he opted to accelerate and deepen the pace of reforms. Government concerns, ranging from the national telephone company Telmex to steel mills and the banks that had been expropriated in the midst of the 1982 crisis, were privatized. Fiscal accounts were streamlined and brought under control, and Mexico joined the United States and Canada in negotiating the North American Free Trade Agreement (NAFTA) as a means of attracting foreign investment and making permanent the reforms that had been enacted. The transformation of the nation's economy and politics, in terms of both structure and expectations, was extraordinary. But the pace and nature of the reforms under Salinas upset many of the critical balances that had held Mexico's political system together for decades. By stripping members of the PRI of many of the benefits of participation, the reforms called into question the terms of the original deal underpinning political stability. First and foremost, deregulation and privatization entailed the loss of opportunity for individual gain and access to wealth among the members of the governing party. But equally important was the fact that electoral competition began to increase and, given the inordinate international visibility that the country had gained, the PRI's practices of vote rigging and fraud became unsustainable. Many PRI candidates began to lose elections, something exceptional in the country's history. The political consequences of this development were enormous, for the president could no longer guarantee that an appointment as candidate actually entailed access to elective office. The question for many members of the PRI was whether it was still attractive to remain disciplined. Furthermore, as opposition candidates increasingly won seats in Congress, the Senate, and municipal and state governments, competitive politics began to take on a life of its own, even if the impact was marginal at the outset. By 1994, when Salinas's term ended, the country's politics had changed beyond recognition.

Even greater shocks were to come. In January 1994, the very day on which NAFTA came into being, an Indian rebellion took the government by surprise. The so-called Zapatistas launched a movement that demanded Salinas's resignation and called on him to oppose free trade. A few months later, in March, the murder of Luis Donaldo Colosio, Salinas's choice as his successor, marked Mexico's first political assassination since the 1920s. The death of Colosio shook the political system, revealing cracks in a political system centered on the president. If the president's choice for successor could be murdered, everything else might be up for grabs as well. His replacement, Ernesto Zedillo (1994–2000), launched a series of policies to try to cope with the new political realities. When he took office, he began negotiations with all of Mexico's political parties to create an independent authority to manage and oversee elections and undertook an initiative designed to transform the Supreme Court into a constitutional court. Zedillo's actions created an environment in which peaceful alternation of parties in government would become possible. Also, after years of electoral disputes, there was finally a mechanism (the autonomous Supreme Court) through which politicians could settle conflicts. Zedillo's inauguration also coincided with yet another devaluation of the peso and the consequent economic crisis, which led to the collapse of most banks. The government failed to develop a coherent policy to rescue the banking system—a failure that would produce extraordinary political effects. A debtors' movement grew out of the crisis, which was quickly co-opted by the PRD, and the National Action Party (PAN) refused to sign on to the subsidies required to rescue the savings of millions of Mexicans.

In the 1997 midterm elections, for the first time in history, the PRI lost control of the Congress, largely because of the economic crisis and the bungled rescue of the banks. Though still the largest party in the 500-member lower house, the PRI ended up with 238 seats against 125 for the PRD, 118 for the center-right PAN, and 19 for the smaller parties. The loss of the PRI majority changed the political dynamics of the country in two ways. First, the president could no longer exercise complete control over the legislative process and several of his bills were defeated—also a first. Second, with the loss of their majority, the members of the PRI themselves began to undergo a change. Party discipline and loyalty weakened and PRI members began airing their views, often in opposition to the president. This change revealed a fissure that had been present since the beginning of the reform process in the 1980s—namely, that the reforms had been crafted largely by the technocrats of the executive branch who had designed them and the PAN, but were passed with the votes of the members of PRI, even when they often disagreed with their

content. This alliance had created the majority necessary for constitutional amendments that PRI legislators had voted for only reluctantly.
Beginning in 1997, and even more so after their loss of the presidency
in 2000, many PRI legislators began to show their true colors: nationalism and populism. Although the PRI was a very diverse party, many
of its members had always subscribed to the notion that the government
should be an all-powerful developmental state that would protect the
weak (including workers and peasants), subsidize industry, and defend
the country from the imperialistic thrust of the United States. This tradition was reclaimed by many a member of the PRI after the 2000
election, bringing them close to the positions of many members of the
PRD.

Both the economic reforms of the late 1980s and early 1990s and the
rapid growth of members of the PAN and the PRD in elective offices
gradually transformed the country's politics. By 2000, a third of Mexico's states and close to half its municipal governments were governed
by opposition parties. By that year, in all but one of the states, the opposition had veto power in the local legislative bodies. Voters had become
confident that elections were being respected and many of them were
willing to exercise the power that that entailed. Hence, even if citizens'
rights remained fairly weak when compared to those of other nations,
Mexican voters were willing to use those they had to the utmost. A
growing number of state races showed extraordinary competition, often
among three candidates. In many cases, PRI candidates won with only
a slim plurality after a majority of the voters had split their votes among
other parties. The stage was set for a very competitive race for the presidency in 2000.

In 2000, Vicente Fox of the PAN was elected to the presidency. In
stark contrast with the average member of the party, Fox was neither a
staunch and unflinching supporter of the party's orthodoxy, nor a candidate willing to launch a campaign aimed at the party's traditional constituencies alone. Actually, many members of the party saw him as a
rogue candidate who had stolen the nomination from under their noses.
Reluctant to convey absolute power to the new president, many of the
same voters who elected Fox voted for a different party for the Congress, which emerged almost evenly split between the PRI and the PAN.
In the lower house, the PRI won 209 seats, the PAN 207, and the PRD
54. The 128-member Senate had 60 representatives from the PRI, 46
from the PAN, and 15 from the PRD. This executive-legislative mismatch created the need for negotiation between the two branches, even
while the nation's institutional structure remained attuned to the old
executive-led system. The paradox of the current political climate is that

a new party holds the presidency, but must coexist with institutions designed for the old system, thereby bringing about the risk of paralysis—precisely the reason why the system was created in the first place. By the same token, it must contend with the by-products of the old system, essentially the noninstitutional actors that emerged after 1968 and refuse to participate in politics through established mechanisms.

What Made Fox's Victory Possible?

Vicente Fox's victory was the result of three factors: the erosion of the legitimacy of the PRI; the existence of a new legal structure for the management of elections that made it impossible for PRI operatives to manipulate the voting process or its results; and Fox's ability to capitalize on discontent and convince the electorate that he offered a different kind of leadership. Each of these factors contributed to the electoral results of 2000, and each represents a different aspect of the political dynamics of Mexico today.

By the 1990s, after decades in power, the PRI had lost both its legitimacy and its capacity to lead the nation. The series of economic crises from 1976 on had eroded the credibility that PRI administrations had earned over the years. Moreover, the government's increasing unwillingness (after 1968) to use force to maintain order had created an environment ripe for change. The PRI had come to life to end the political violence that had characterized Mexico in the early decades of the twentieth century; at that time, attaining peace and stability had been an accomplishment in and of itself. Seventy years later, however, the needs of the people had changed and the PRI had proven itself incapable of responding to their demands.

From the late 1920s to the late 1960s, PRI governments had combined orthodoxy in the economic arena (maintaining the fiscal accounts in order and keeping inflation under control) and ruthlessness in the political sphere (using violence whenever it was perceived to be necessary). Nineteen sixty-eight was a watershed year on both counts. Although the administrations that followed remained harsh in their style of political management, they shied away from using the police to contain demonstrations or to control violent movements. Once it became clear that governments were unwilling to use force to control riots or hinder lawless groups from blocking major highways or city streets, the decline in PRI power and credibility began in earnest. On the economic front, the rapid increase in public spending post-1970 succeeded in appeasing those constituencies that might challenge the government (particularly students and the middle classes), but it also created an inflationary environment that undermined economic stability and brought about a series of crises that impoverished millions of Mexicans. In retrospect, it was this dual shift in the nature of PRI administrations—away from the use of violence and away from fiscal prudence—that made it possible, thirty years later, for a democratic opening to occur.

The economic reforms of the 1980s and 1990s spelled an end to the power of the PRI. Economic reforms entail changes in the political environment. In Mexico, where behind every regulation lies a vested interest, each of the steps pursued by administrations from 1982 through 2000 brought about a gradual redefinition of the structure of power. By giving up control of major parastatal companies (such as Telmex, the banks, or the steel companies), the government lost its prime vehicles for allocating the spoils of corruption within the PRI. By deregulating the import and foreign investment regimes, it undermined the interests of local producers, unions, and political clusters, all of which had prospered through subsidies, import permits, and the pricing power provided by the absence of competition. By allowing free electoral competition, the government eroded its ability to reward PRI politicians with electoral office. Gradually, as the reforms unfolded, the structure of power, in particular that of the president, declined.

NAFTA played a major role in this process, although in a way that is often misunderstood in the United States. NAFTA was, to a large extent, the *end* of the process of reform. It was not meant to launch new reforms, but to confer permanence on those that had been enacted in the previous years. Once NAFTA came into being, the government failed to create the conditions that would have been necessary to transform the economy as a whole (such as investing heavily in infrastructure, transforming the agricultural sector, upgrading the educational system, and developing a foundation for technological development). Hence, one of the traits of NAFTA is that its positive impacts are concentrated in a number of regions and sectors of the economy where exports have thrived, jobs have been created, and salaries have increased above the median, while it has negatively affected virtually all the country's traditional producers that failed to adjust to competition from imports. By the same token, the very fact that the government accepted restrictions on its own behavior and allowed NAFTA to place Mexico on the world stage meant that new political freedoms became available to Mexicans. Fearing international repercussions, the Mexican government could no longer repress a political movement (as Salinas found early in 1994 with the Zapatistas). Also, the very fact that consumers found competition to be beneficial in terms of choice constituted an incentive for competitive politics elsewhere. In this sense, many of NAFTA's greatest critics, among them nongovernmental organizations (NGOs) and prodemocracy groups, were also its greatest beneficiaries.

Although the forces leading to the erosion of the PRI's legitimacy had been under way for several decades, the first tangible sign of the party's decline was its defeat in the 1997 midterm elections. Though the opposition parties tried—and usually failed—to build an anti-PRI coalition during the legislative term that followed, the more significant event was the rebellion against the party leadership by its traditional members, those *pristas* that had always supported the president. Having concluded that the benefits of party discipline no longer warranted its costs, it was they who opposed further reforms and it was they who defeated the president at every turn. The *pristas* opposed reform not only because it undermined their political interests, but also on ideological grounds. This challenge clearly signaled the kind of difficulties any future non-PRI administration would face. Many members of the PRI, the same legislators who had voted for reforms even if they opposed them, began to argue that the only way to recover control of the Congress was through the dismantling of those reforms. This sentiment inevitably deepened after 2000. The PRI ended up losing support and legitimacy because it was not able to deliver, but also because it represented a past most Mexicans wanted to break free of. What few were able to predict in 2000 is that the issue of legitimacy affected not only the PRI, but also many of the things it has been associated with, including the reforms themselves.

The second factor that made it possible for Vicente Fox to win the elections of 2000 was the new Federal Electoral Institute (IFE) and its sister institution, the Federal Electoral Tribunal. Both were born in 1996 out of negotiations among all the political parties after years of fighting over electoral fraud and manipulation. Endless electoral disagreements had meant that political parties would often spend most of their funds after election day, which was when the real negotiations began. A series of agreements on electoral reform, first in 1993 and then in 1996, ended up producing a basic structure to which all political forces unanimously subscribed and which became a turning point in the country's politics. Though many leading members of the PRI opposed the reforms, Zedillo made full use of his vast presidential powers to get it through the congressional process. Even then, many *pristas* realized that the lack of credibility of the electoral process was becoming too costly for the party's own good. Few thought the PRI would lose as a result.

The IFE and the Federal Electoral Tribunal introduced two crucial changes. One was that the administration of elections would henceforth be the responsibility of an independent and autonomous entity with

broad powers to rule over the entire process and impose san[
offenders. The tribunal would have equally broad powers to s ....
putes and rule whenever disagreements ensued. Thus, for the first time
in decades, elections were taken out of the realm of PRI influence,
opening up the electoral process to outright competition.

The new electoral laws also changed another significant aspect of
Mexican politics: once the electoral process ceased to be subject to
manipulation and fraud by PRI operatives, the points of contention
became more substantive. Previously, elections had served as the meta-
phorical lightning rod that captured the key issue in dispute among the
political parties: access to power. Once the parties had moved the electoral process into a neutral and independent arena, the subject of dispute
shifted away from elections and toward a range of more substantive
issues. Some of these were legitimate sources of contention, such as the
allocation of budgets, but others involved illegitimate actions, such as
the use of violent demonstrations, highway closures, or mafia-style
union threats, to inhibit open and public debate.

The end of the era of disputed elections through noninstitutional
means did not merely open up the possibility of victory by an opposition party; it also changed the nature of political conflict in Mexico. In
the past, such conflict had remained within the political apparatus (i.e.,
within the PRI and its networks); after 1997, conflict came out into the
open. And whereas in the past the PRI had instruments that allowed it to
control or at least contain those conflicts, today's institutions are not
adequate for that task.

The erosion of the PRI's legitimacy and the autonomous management of elections were both instrumental in bringing about the PRI's
defeat, but a third factor was equally relevant: the role of Vicente Fox.
Capitalizing on the momentum that had begun to build after the 1997
midterm elections, Fox developed a strategy that steamrolled him through
his party's nomination process and through the campaign to election
day. Fox had emerged as a leading figure within the party after the 1982
expropriation-of-the-banks debacle, when a major businessman who
was then president of the business council (CCE) as well as a future
PAN presidential candidate, Manuel Clouthier, drew him and many
other disgruntled businesspeople into the political arena. Fox became a
member of Congress and then ran for the governorship of his native
state of Guanajuato. That election was marred with fraud and Fox
launched a major drive to force the PRI to concede. Eventually, a negotiated solution called for a third individual to be appointed interim governor and a new election was scheduled. Fox won outright, his stature
greatly enhanced. He used his years as governor to campaign around the

nation and to develop a political team to eventually run a campaign. Breaking with tradition, he included in his team disgruntled members of other parties as well as individuals who were not appreciated by the traditionalist PAN rank and file. Nonetheless, many inside his party realized that to win the presidency they would need a true leader that people outside the party could join with, so they helped lay the groundwork for his eventual nomination. This was no small task, since among the measures needed was a constitutional amendment (to allow a Mexican born of non-Mexican parents to be president) without which Fox could not have been a candidate. Fox announced his candidacy immediately following the midterm elections, three years before the critical day in July 2000. A master at marketing, the new candidate designed a program to address virtually every constituency around the nation; opened negotiations with other opposition parties, mainly the PRD; and, despite being an outsider in his own party, by late 1999 had secured the nomination as presidential candidate. Both his political skills and his ability to lead had proven extremely effective.

The key element in Fox's victory was the fact that he offered the prospect of a peaceful and conflict-free political transition to an electorate that desperately wanted an alternative to the PRI but did not find Cuauhtémoc Cárdenas and the PRD's perceived radicalism appealing. Fox understood the electorate perfectly, offering a guarantee of continuity to those who desired it and the promise of change to those who were fed up with the existing system. As a candidate free from decision-making responsibilities, he was able to adjust his rhetoric to each audience. Ultimately, he developed the notion of the "useful vote" to encourage those who wanted a change in party of the presidency to vote for him even if they voted for their preferred party for Congress. This occurred after a particularly dire performance in a debate one afternoon toward the end of the campaign period where he appeared inflexible and dogmatic, a day that then became known as "Black Tuesday." With virtually all the pundits assuming Fox's campaign was doomed, he turned his ill-spoken words into a slogan and went on to defeat the PRI.

Fox had two additional advantages. First, in a country of *caudillos* (strong leaders), his demeanor and charisma were closer to what people perceived to be necessary for the presidency than that of Francisco Labastida, the PRI contender. Second, Labastida, an experienced apparatchik, ran a traditional and lackluster campaign at a time when most voters were demanding change. In fact, most polls showed that more than 60 percent of voters were looking for an alternative to PRI rule, a figure that was quite close to the actual electoral result, if one adds together Fox's and Cárdenas's votes. It was Labastida's failure to recognize this fact that led him to commit a strategic error by not seeking to divide his opposition. Fox, on the other hand, grasped the desire for change and looked desperately for ways of reaching beyond the traditional PAN coalition, which was too narrow to deliver the necessary votes. At the end of the day, Fox proved himself a master at understanding Mexicans' needs and ended up riding the wave of their disillusionment with corruption, crime, and lack of accountability.

Fox's successful campaign planted the seeds of many of his difficulties today. The coalition that he assembled to win the presidency—a broad grouping of everyone who wanted a non-PRI president—was largely unacceptable to his party. (In reality, the very traditional leadership and constituency of the PAN has generally preferred doctrinal purity to electoral victory.) Fox's approach was anathema to most PAN politicians, many of whom do not identify with the president and at times even vote against his bills. (Some *panistas* now claim that "this is Fox's *sexenio*, and the next one will be ours.") Also, the complexity of that same coalition has translated into an incoherent cabinet with contradictory priorities and agendas where, in the absence of a strong coordinating mechanism, each of the supporting constituencies feels it has a right-of-way through "its" member of the cabinet. Fox's approach when building his cabinet was based not on a plan to govern effectively, but on his perceived need to keep his various constituencies close-by.

Once in office, he did not develop an effective coordinating mechanism for such a diverse cabinet and, for two years, was reluctant to make changes even in light of infighting and ineffectiveness. Another of Fox's difficulties stems from the fact that he promised change but never defined it. Even worse, once his administration was inaugurated, he assumed that everyone, including the Congress, would follow his lead and accede to his priorities simply because of the democratic feat he had just accomplished. His contradictory messages and campaign promises (such as to deliver 7 percent growth and to eradicate corruption and crime) became competing priorities in a fledging administration that has found it difficult to define its goals, let alone accomplish them. Finally, the affinity for marketing over substance that served Fox so well during the campaign has become a major handicap now that he is president. His tendency to permanently raise expectations has become too heavy a burden, since nothing Fox accomplishes will ever be perceived as being close to what he has promised.

More than halfway through its tenure, the Fox administration has little to show for its efforts. The economy has remained stable but, absent a strong source of demand from the U.S. economy, growth has been left wanting. Unemployment has increased, although marginally. Most important, none of the president's significant bills (on electricity reform, fiscal reform, labor reform, or Indian rights) has been approved in the legislature. If anything, crime has increased and the president's popularity has decreased. The cabinet remains a source of infighting and ineffectiveness rather than action. All in all, the first non-PRI administration has shattered more expectations than it has satisfied.

What Changed?

With the victory of Vicente Fox, Mexican politics experienced a profound revolution. The PRI, which had governed Mexico for seventy years, had operated under a simple premise: loyalty and discipline in exchange for benefits. The party had fostered the development of organizations in virtually every walk of life, from agriculture to labor unions, business interests, the military, and the middle classes. Even garbage collectors were represented. Every group had a place inside the party, but always in exchange for its loyalty. Much more than a political party created to compete in elections, the PRI was a mechanism for exercising political control, a broad organization with tentacles reaching into every area of the economy and society. PRI officials solved problems for their constituents, helped their organizations prosper, and enriched the leaders of unions and other entities. Whenever a Mexican wanted something from government—and government was ubiquitous—he or she had to resort to the PRI. The network of controls that developed within the party became a prime source of power for the president, who was also the PRI's leader.

When the link between the PRI and the presidency was broken in 2000, everything changed. Not only was the presidency now held by a leader of a party other than the PRI, but the political system as a whole underwent a revolution. The office of the presidency proved to be relatively weak in constitutional terms, while the PRI began to disintegrate in the absence of a source of benefits—typically, access to power and corruption—that the close connection with the presidency had provided. From this perspective, the defeat of the PRI at the hands of Vicente Fox was tantamount to a radical shift in political power in Mexico. But while the reality of power changed, the nation's political institutions did not. And the result is disarray.

The old political system operated around two institutions: the presidency and the PRI. Each depended on the other to make the country work. The two institutions were integrated through an extraordinary network of organizations that served to channel demands, settle disputes, advance special interests, negotiate benefits, and service a huge system of controls that helped maintain political stability. In order to achieve its objectives, the PRI worked in conjunction with the government and the presidency. The government's expenditures were closely tied to the party's needs, and vice versa. The presidency used the PRI to advance its goals, the foremost of which was to maintain control and discipline over organizations, regions, or individuals. The party, in turn, used its close relationship to the government to convey to its constituencies that it was an effective representative of their interests. The goal of this system was to develop, nurture, and sustain the party's legitimacy, from the largest transactions to the smallest details: the party was there when a company needed an import permit, just as it was there when someone required a driver's license.

Both the party and the presidency had strong incentives to cooperate. Through the decades in which the legislature was dominated by the PRI, disciplined voting was the name of the game. By voting for the president's bills, party members enjoyed a vast array of benefits, including access to power and the spoils of corruption. The party served as an exceptional vehicle to punish and reward individuals. Individual legislators, in theory representing the voters, would vote with the president, knowing full well that discipline would always be rewarded. Party discipline made it possible for the president to advance the administration's policies, impose decisions whenever necessary, and make them stick.

Yet this was not a dictatorship in which the president operated at will. The relationship between the PRI and the presidency was complex and often cumbersome, and the multiplicity of interests involved extraordinary. The president exercised power through permanent negotiation, "pulling and hauling," and considerable conflict. But even if the specific interests of the party and the presidency did not always coincide, their broad interests and incentives were perfectly aligned. Political and economic developments from 1968 on, however, set in motion the end to this symbiotic relationship between president and party.

The old political system began to be transformed after 1968. Until then, every time the president, the party, or the system had been, or perceived itself to be, challenged, it had acted forcefully: while favoring co-optation, it was always ready to resort to repression. That is why the government reacted so strongly to the student movement. But this would be the last time it could do so. The state's violent actions had enormous consequences. The students had not challenged the system's power, but its legitimacy, and the subsequent repression had led to a severe loss of legitimacy. After this, the government ceased to resort to repression; as long as nobody challenged its legitimacy, dissent would be tolerated, even financed. This led to the growth and development of a new phenomenon: the surge of noninstitutional entities and interests around the country.

While Mexico's political institutions have experienced a profound transformation, the noninstitutional side of the nation's politics has not. Organizations representing vested interests—unions of workers in monopoly sectors (such as electricity and oil), violence-prone students, land invaders, illegal taxi drivers—continue to operate as they always have, including through their connections to the most reactionary and traditional members of the PRI and the PRD. The strength of these groups stems not from elections, but from raw power. They can control facilities that are central to the functioning of the economy (as do workers at Mexico's oil company, PEMEX, or the utility company, CFE). They can challenge law-enforcement agencies (as in the case of the machete-wielding opponents of a new airport for Mexico City). They can shut down the national university and similar institutions with a strike. They can bring large cities, major roads, or key production facilities to a halt through threats or physical obstruction. These groups have their own interests and dynamics, but often enjoy a symbiotic relationship with members of the PRI or the PRD, or both. Each uses the other in the pursuit of its interests.

The student movement also caused ruptures within the party, and the government found itself incapable of making decisions, particularly on the allocation of funds to competing constituencies. It ended up spending on all of them under the rationale that inflation would be a lesser evil than political confrontation. Government spending became the chief avenue to sustaining the old political coalition inside the PRI. When these policies finally led to a major financial collapse and recession, first in 1976 and then in 1982, the system experienced a second fracture. The price of twelve years of economic populism was paid during the 1980s—a decade-long recession during which standards of living fell as Mexico's fiscal accounts were gradually brought back under control.

In the 1980s and 1990s, three successive administrations attempted to control the economic fallout from these crises and establish the foundation for economic development in an era of globalization. Their main objective was to reform the economy and restore growth without losing the party's grip on power. But the economic reforms were fundamentally in conflict with the nature of the PRI and its system of control. Liberalization of imports and deregulation meant the dismantling of government control over permits and licenses, and restricted access to benefits and special favors. By using the party's structure and system of control to advance economic reforms, the presidency ended up weakening the party, as it removed the instruments that had traditionally served to reward loyalty and punish insubordination. Without the reforms, however, the economy would have collapsed and the system would have failed anyway. In this sense, the reforms were an attempt by the executive (and against the PRI) to restore stability and retain as much power as possible.

In hindsight, it is clear that governments during this period were not fully cognizant of the political implications of reform. They were not trying to transform Mexican society; their only aim was to make the economy work. Reforming governments often pursued contradictory policies: they wanted to liberalize, but not lose control; they aimed to create competition, but often transferred government assets to their cronies in the private sector; they talked about a modern economy, but relied on an old political system to launch the reforms. Some of the reforms, in particular some of the privatizations, were marred by all of these problems simultaneously. Inadequate reforms led inexorably to serious problems; one example is the ill-conceived privatization of the banking system in the early 1990s, which then, after the devaluation of 1994, had to be rescued at the extreme cost of some 12 percent of gross domestic product (GDP). While reform may have been necessary, in practice its policies were often clouded and sometimes corrupt.

Although the old political system was weakened by the loss of its traditional instruments of control, until the late 1990s party discipline remained very much alive. Criticism of the president, impossible during the heyday of PRI dominance, became more common, but when it came to voting nobody wavered. The PRI's loss of its congressional majority in 1997 signaled the beginning of the end of its rule. Not only could the opposition now strive to impose its preferences, so could disgruntled members of the PRI. For PRI legislators, the loss of their majority was tantamount to being liberated. From then on, they no longer needed to accept the president's dictates. By the same token, they also lost the means to settle disputes among themselves and, conceivably, the mechanism to nominate a presidential candidate in the future.

The elections of July 2000 further transformed the political arena. By severing the ties between the party and the presidency, the electorate deprived the president of the instruments with which he had traditionally governed. The president could no longer engage in systematic negotiations with the members of a dominant party and exercise leverage over the legislature and society. The combination of a rebellious Congress—most of whose members adamantly rejected negotiating with the president and repudiated any attempt to influence their vote— and a much less powerful presidency rendered gridlock unavoidable.

Everything may have changed for Mexico's politicians, but little is different for its citizens. Legislators are free from the old system of discipline and accountability; they now have an impact on policy and can derail the president's bills if they choose. Ordinary citizens, however, have little connection to their representatives and virtually no impact on their votes. Other than no longer being subjected to the whims of a very strong president (no mean feat), citizens have won little leverage over politicians. Because legislators are not allowed to run for immediate reelection, there is limited accountability to the voters. (The prohibition against consecutive terms is found in the 1917 Constitution and is a consequence of the abuses of President Porfirio Diaz's long rule from 1876 to 1910.) Legislators benefit little from catering to the voters, so they don't. Members of Congress, once accountable to the president alone, are today accountable to their party leaders, who exercise tremendous influence over their future careers. The citizens these legislators purportedly represent have neither access to nor influence over their representatives.

These facts have transformed the fundamental structures of Mexico's government. Constitutionally, the Mexican presidency is much weaker than that of most other nations in the hemisphere. The Mexican constitution grants the president relatively few powers compared to those of nations such as Argentina, Chile, or even the United States. Unlike the case in some countries, Mexico's president does not have exclusive rights to introduce legislation, does not have powers to impose temporary decrees, and does not have powers to veto legislation. Academic research comparing the executive powers of twenty-three countries (the Shugart-Haggard Index) shows Mexico with a score of one on a scale of zero to six, as compared to six for Argentina, four for Brazil, and two for the United States.[1] Mexico's presidency was powerful not because of the attributes granted to it by the constitution, but because of the network of controls afforded by its relationship to the PRI. Through both the party and a series of extralegal powers (the so-called meta-constitutional powers, such as the system of loyalties and the unwritten rules of the game), Mexico's presidents were able to exert extremely tight control over the nation for many decades. Once the presidency was divorced from the PRI, the reality of power changed dramatically.

The political consequences of this new reality can be seen in the inability of the Fox administration to advance its agenda. The source of the problem is not so much the quality of that agenda, but changes in the political system. Unlike his predecessors, Fox cannot impose his preferences on Congress. Everything must be negotiated; however, the incentives that once encouraged compromise and agreement are now gone. Only those issues that are noncontroversial and those that must be dealt with, such as the budget, have been passed; none of the president's other major bills has advanced. Also, the power that was formerly concentrated in the office of the president has migrated to other parts of the federal government and to state governors, who have become the standard bearers of their political parties. The PRI remains the largest party in the country and controls the largest number of governorships. Time will tell whether it can survive its loss of 2000, but it is certain that the old political system cannot be re-created.

These changes create opportunities for the development of a democratic polity that were inconceivable only a few years ago. They also pose the extraordinary challenge of developing a new political system that is geared toward the benefit of the individual citizen—even today, something foreign to Mexico's political culture—rather than to the clique that inherited its privileges from the Revolution of 1910. Furthermore, such a system could only be developed with the concurrence of the very political forces that today oppose any further diminution of their own powers. In other words, the political system of old was created to maintain control and stability while benefiting the members of the so-called revolutionary family. A future political system would have to operate around the citizen while developing the checks and balances necessary for effective governance and representation. It is not clear how this can be accomplished, given the tremendous political fragmentation that characterizes the country; the existence of an electoral system that favors the creation, albeit not the growth, of small political parties; and the lack of committed constituencies to one or another party. In stark contrast with the distant past, when the PRI could muster huge majorities and the allegiance of most Mexicans, more than 60 percent of the electorate today is uncommitted. Voters can easily shift from one party to another, a factor that underlines the existing electoral volatility.

Many Mexicans assume that the diminished power of the president is due to a lack of political skill on the part of President Fox. Although his inexperience may certainly be a factor, as the cabinet's dynamics show, the issue goes well beyond personalities. President Fox simply does not enjoy the power that his predecessors have had. Unless Mexico's political parties are able to develop a new power alignment (such as an absolute majority in both houses of Congress) or, better yet, a system that includes representation based on reelection and other effective mechanisms of accountability, the current power configuration is one that is especially prone to gridlock. Although the Congress has been able to pass more bills than its predecessors, it has shied away from undertaking anything controversial. This includes most of the economic reform bills proposed by the current administration, the provisions of which are anathema to the PRI and the PRD either because they affect some of their core constituencies, such as the unions of oil and electricity workers, or on ideological grounds. Although the need for a major political overhaul is widely recognized, there is little consensus over its nature or content. Everyone agrees that the ultimate objective of reform should be to create an effective and accountable government, but every politician and pundit defines such a potential reform in a different way. No one is ready to take the first step: Mexico has no James Madison and no Federalist Papers at a time when they are most needed.

Political power has migrated away from the presidency to, first and foremost, the Congress. The Congress has become the center for political negotiations as well as a major source of gridlock. Since the members of Congress cannot run for consecutive terms, they have little or no incentive to negotiate with the president or listen to their constituents. By the same token, the absence of reelection and the fact that political campaigns are (or are supposed to be) funded by the public purse, means that lobbyists have a difficult time gaining access to the corridors of power in the legislature. Unless special interests resort to the outright buying of congressional votes (which often happens), members of Congress can remain both uninformed as well as distant from the electorate. This situation produces an odd result: the Congress has seen its powers dramatically increased, but it is no more accountable to the voters than it ever was. Hence, within the usually lax rules of party discipline (which vary from party to party), each member of Congress is basically free to pursue his or her own agenda, be it personal or partisan. In the absence of controls from above, democracy has become a boon for the members of Congress and their leaders at the expense of citizens and of the president. Paradoxically, because of the fact that the Mexican Congress mixes direct and proportional representation, even if reelection were allowed, in the current context it would likely serve only to preserve the power of a few individuals without altering the political structure of the country. In fact, many members of Congress have expressed their intention of modifying this historical provision in order to shield themselves from popular pressure by being elected through proportional representation.

Power has also migrated to the media. Once merely a conduit for government propaganda, the media has become a critical political actor. Years of self-censorship (exercised in exchange for benefits and privileges for the owners or publishers) have given way to an era in which media outlets act as unruly, uncompromising, and aggressive political players pushing their own agendas and interests and only sometimes providing news and analysis. Not all media outlets are equally at fault, but most depart from the critical role that their peers perform in democratic societies, such as being a source of objective news and information or undertaking investigative reporting and analysis. Still, a free media, even if unruly, is better than what existed previously. The hope is that, as other institutions mature, so will the media.

Probably the most important emerging new actors in the country's politics are the governors and some municipal leaders who have seen their power vastly increased in a number of ways. In the first place, the structure of controls once used by the PRI to discipline them has vanished. These actors are now owners of a significant part of the political process, often exercising influence over their state's representatives in Congress by providing them with funds and offering employment when their terms are over—all to advance the governors' political interests and careers (most governors are now presidential hopefuls). In addition, governors and municipal presidents have seen their budgets skyrocket as the result of ever-larger direct transfers from the federal budget without any means of making them accountable for the use of these funds. Governors prefer to raise money directly from the federal government than from their own state residents, for the accountability of those funds is very lax and, in this new era, easy to politicize. Hence, fiscal decentralization with no accountability entails grave risks for the long-term stability of the government's finances. In 1990, governors had spending authority and control over 52 cents of each peso spent by the federal government, while today they spend 1.68 pesos per peso spent by the central government. In other words, the governors now receive three times as many funds from the federal government as they did before, and their relative power has increased dramatically.[2] The result is that the federal budget has been ransacked, with governors enjoying vast resources and tremendous discretion in spending, and citizens once again remaining on the sidelines. It is no wonder that many of these new monies have ended up being used to pay for luxury cars, rather than sewers, education, or roads.

The political parties, as well as a myriad of independent and autonomous entities, such as the IFE and the central bank, have become critical players in the country's politics. In the economic sphere, institutions such as the Banco de México can limit the arbitrary powers of the government and the Congress. (This is the one area where the PRI governments of the 1980s and 1990s did create a network, albeit a small one, of effective oversight institutions.) Whether in elections or monetary policy, there exist a series of entities that are independent and have proven their worth over the past few years of post-PRI rule. The same goes for the Supreme Court.

The Supreme Court, and the judiciary in general, is quickly becoming a central arbiter of disputes within the political system. After gaining both autonomy as well as powers to review the constitutionality of laws, the Supreme Court has inched its way through political conflicts among politicians and levels of government (individual citizens have no access to the court). In a political system characterized by weak institutions and many legal vacuums, constitutional controversies are becoming more frequent. The Supreme Court has played a key, albeit extremely controversial, role in defining the limits of presidential authority. What it has not done is to take on the defense of individual rights, a role that its counterparts in the United States or Spain are famous for. Even if its role has been controversial, the court has become a credible dispute-settling mechanism among all political actors. In fact, the brightest aspect of Mexican politics today is that, despite a high level of conflict, most controversies and political disputes are being channeled through the judiciary. Eighty years ago, such conflicts would have been settled in the street.

The Meaning and Implications
of the New Political Reality

Since the 1980s, Mexico has undergone a series of institutional changes, particularly in the electoral realm, that gradually liberalized the country's politics and provided breathing room for a tired political system. These changes culminated in the election of the nation's first non-PRI president, a development that seemed to signal the full emergence of Mexican democracy. Everything seemed possible now that the PRI—allegedly the chief stumbling block to progress—had been removed from the nation's most powerful office. But these historic developments also raised expectations beyond the realm of the possible.

Many believed that the Fox government would enjoy a "democratic bonus," making possible a series of major agreements among the parties that would fundamentally change Mexico's political institutions. The idea was that all Mexicans, whether they had voted for Fox or not, would join in an extraordinary democratic feast favoring dramatic changes and opening a new era for the nation. But the bonus never materialized, leading to major miscalculations on the part of Fox's transition team, the lack of an effective strategy for dealing with the Congress (the majority of which was held by the combination of opposition parties), and the stalemate that now characterizes the nation's politics. The Fox administration spent almost two years debating within itself whether to approach the PRI or to oppose it as a means to pass legislation; in the process, it succeeded only in alienating the members of its own party, most of whom were in any event unwilling to work with the new president. The political approach proved to be mistaken, while the policy differences, both within the cabinet as well as between the government and the parties in Congress, made it impossible to reach compromises. Above all, the Fox administration did not develop a coherent strategy to deal with the members of Congress, independent of the policy content of its initiatives. Given the structural problems described above, it is not clear that a different strategy would have produced a better outcome, but it does appear that the new president squandered his political capital quickly and without having much to show for it.

Fox's victory took place in an institutional and legal vacuum. While the party wielding power had changed, the old institutional structures remained the same. But instead of the traditional system of PRI rule, where the executive and legislature operated as one, Mexico now had to rely on constitutional provisions that were inadequate to bring about effective cooperation between the two branches of government. The creation of new institutional arrangements would require two-thirds majorities in Congress (because most of these would involve constitutional amendments), something difficult to achieve with a relatively even split in congressional seats between the PRI and the PAN.

Although the reform of Mexico's electoral system had been under way for several years, it was the 2000 elections that marked the beginning of the nation's true political transition. While formal institutions such as political parties, the Congress, and the Supreme Court began to adjust to the new reality right away, informal groupings did not. The vested interests and noninstitutional players that had thrived outside the rule of law have continued to use extortion and other extralegal means of accomplishing their goals as though nothing had changed. Their continued existence poses an anomaly for a political system that aims to be democratic and poses challenges to both presidential authority and the stability of the system at large.

Different institutions are adjusting in different ways. The Supreme Court has grown stronger as it plays a crucial role in breaking the deadlock between the executive and the Congress and in defining the limits of presidential power in a nation where tradition had created a virtually unaccountable presidency. Congressional politics, too, are dedicated toward weakening an already frail presidency. Nowhere, however, is there an emerging force dedicated to restructuring the institutional arrangements inherited from Mexico's past.

At the same time, each of the vested interests that had thrived under the PRI is attempting to maintain or consolidate its power. Unions with monopoly positions, particularly those associated with government-owned entities such as Petróleos Mexicanos (PEMEX), the main electric utility, Comisión Federal de Electricidad (CFE), and the teacher's union, have become aggressive players in the country's politics in an effort to preserve the benefits gained during PRI rule. Their efforts undermine one of Fox's chief goals—to increase the competitiveness of the economy as a means to raising the standards of living of the population.

In addition to these well-known entities are special interests that challenge not only the government but the development of a peaceful and legitimate civil society. Mexico has a growing and diverse civil society, with groups active in areas like human rights, the environment, and support for the poor. They participate in political debate and act within the existing institutional structure, thereby strengthening the nation's political stability. But there is another group of noninstitutional entities that operate outside the rule of law. They include guerrilla groups such as the Zapatistas and its more violent cousins, the Popular Revolutionary Army (EPR) and its splinters based in the mountains of Oaxaca and Guerrero; violent organizations such as Los Pancho Villas, which control some areas of Mexico City and live off both crime and the indirect subsidies they receive from the local government that tries to buy them off; the machete-wielding activists that derailed the Zedillo administration's development project in Tepoztlán and now the Fox administration's planned Mexico City airport; organizations representing land invaders in various parts of the country; taxi drivers operating without licenses; student organizations such as the one that paralyzed the National University with a year-long strike; and other gangster-type organizations. Some of these organizations may be related to drugs and many are either linked to or part of organized crime.

Some elements within Mexico's political parties, which are formally part of the legitimate institutional sector, have access to these noninstitutional organizations and cater to both sides. In Congress or in a partisan context, they participate in open, legal, and competitive politics; at the same time they will deal with and make use of illegitimate or illegal organizations. For example, the protesters who opposed Mexico City's new airport did so through illegal actions, like blockades of major arteries and threats with their machetes, while enjoying the unofficial sponsorship or backing of members of the PRI and the PRD, both of which were interested in undermining the president's legitimacy. In this case, elements of two of the major political parties were willing to resort to violent protest to advance their short-term interests.

The party that has had the most difficulty adjusting to the new, post-2000 reality is undoubtedly the PRI. The party that was always associated with governing suddenly found itself leaderless as well as clueless. In its heyday, the president had nurtured both leadership and a sense of direction. Now there was no natural leader. Infighting and competition ensued, while political and policy differences, previously glossed over, suddenly sprang into the open. While maintaining a semblance of unity, particularly when voting in the Congress, the party has now become a collection of groupings, usually fighting for power with the others. But beyond these, the party is focused on the past. Although the party accepted its defeat in 2000 and has participated in Congress as a legitimate player, most of its members are waging an old war over the question of who bears responsibility for the PRI's loss. Traditional party members contend that it was not they, the so-called historical PRI, who lost the election, but rather the technocrats who were responsible for the reforms of the 1980s and 1990s. From their vantage point, the presidents who presided over the reforms—de la Madrid, Salinas, and Zedillo—as well as the technocratic members of their respective cabinets, pursued policies that ended up producing the party's defeat. In this view, the PRI's loss of the presidency was due not to the mistakes of various PRI administrations, nor to the economic crises of the past thirty years, nor to the abuse of power and corruption, nor even to the fatigue of the voters. The defeat was due to the way the party's technocrats ran the country, especially their abandonment of the linked policies of nationalism, protection for domestic producers, subsidies, greater government involvement in economic matters, and a more distant relationship with the United States. Those who sustain this line of thinking assume that the voters will turn back to the PRI as soon as they have an opportunity, and they are willing to do anything necessary, whether in the institutional or noninstitutional realm of politics, to defeat Fox's agenda.

There are few precedents to guide Mexico during this vast and profound transformation. The closest analogy may come from Russia, where a monopoly party also had to be dismantled and a new institutional structure developed. In stark contrast with nations such as Spain or Chile, where the outgoing government planned a course of action and developed institutions for the nascent democracy, in Mexico there is no plan, no course to guide politicians. Beyond the 1996 reforms that established the terms of electoral competition and the settlement of disputes, there was nothing else to go on—no agreement on how the institutional structure should be adjusted, no rules of the game to deal with the new legislative-executive tension. In Spain, there was the king, the courts, and the legislative branch, all ready to work in a new political situation. Something like that existed in Chile. In Mexico, the old institutions remained in place and there is little incentive for members of Congress to dismantle them. It may take another major victory of a non-PRI candidate for this to begin to change. The legal and institutional vacuum, combined with an inexperienced administration, a harsh opposition, and the presence of noninstitutional players on the sidelines, has created an extremely volatile political environment. And there is an additional complicating factor: most members of the PRD claim that democracy will be attained only if and when they win the presidency. Even though its numbers in the Congress are very small (20 percent of the Congress and less of the Senate), the PRD thrives in its opposition role and has an extraordinary ability to define the political agenda. Though the PRD embodies several currents, many of them with contradictory interests and objectives, it has been remarkably successful at embarrassing members of the two larger political parties. By challenging them on their neoliberal agenda—used as a negative code word with the Mexican public—the PRD has developed a political weight that vastly exceeds its numerical strength.

As in many other nations, the speed of change in the nation's politics over the past thirty years has created major gaps in perception. One gap is generational. An older generation, accustomed to the stability provided by PRI rule, has had difficulty adjusting to the volatility and gridlock that are the order of the day. Many who think this way are natural PRI constituents. A slightly younger generation remembers the era in which authority meant fear and lived through the expropriation of the banks, inflation, mismanaged privatizations, and one economic crisis after another. They tend to see the current situation as the lesser of two evils, neither as bad as the authoritarian governments that led to 1968, nor the chaotic years of inflation and stagnation that followed. Younger generations that have only known years of economic crises can hardly distinguish the economic reforms and their consequences from the political changes that have taken place.

Yet most Mexicans celebrated the electoral defeat of the PRI. Whether or not they had voted for Fox, most were tired of the PRI, even if at some point they had seen its virtues. The very fact that votes counted and were counted constituted a true revolution for a population that had become accustomed to being cheated on a permanent basis. The makings of a democratic political culture may very well have been born in this process. But it is too soon to reach such a conclusion. Mexicans are as much heirs to the authoritarian past as they are to the culture of dependency that the PRI system nurtured. They are as prone to demand that their needs be satisfied as they are to understanding the trade-off between rights and responsibilities implicit in democratic politics.

While it would be wrong to suggest that Mexicans have not changed since election day 2000, it would be equally improper to claim that they have become born-again democrats. Many of the old ways remain very much a part of their daily routine. There is virtually no respect for traffic signs and rules, and one still finds public parking spaces for "rent" on any busy street. People do as much as they can to avoid paying taxes, but nonetheless demand services from the government and protest loudly whenever the government proposes a fee or tax for a given benefit. But it would be difficult to expect a more profound cultural change. Two factors conspire against that. First, the president has largely failed to break away from the policies of his predecessors. Even though Fox emerged as president from the first legitimate election in modern history, his administration has maintained similar policies, some for good, others for bad. One unfortunate continuity is the government's view of the police as a repressive force—an attitude that makes it difficult to develop means of enforcing the law, something necessary in any truly democratic society. The Fox government, heir to years of criticism of PRI rule, cannot see itself using its authority, even against lawless groups. Second, the lives of Mexicans have actually changed very little since Fox became president. The economy remains weak, citizens' relationship with the government is basically unchanged, their rights remain the same, access to the judiciary is essentially blocked by red tape and ineffectiveness, and members of Congress are unconcerned about their welfare, at least on an individual basis. Democracy may have radically altered the political structure, but other than making it safe for everyone to laugh at the politicians—an important, if minor, measure of democracy—it has had little impact on daily life. A recent example is a referendum called by the government of the Federal District in order to determine whether to build a second level over one of the city's main arteries. There was no explanation of the need for the new road, no arguments about its pros and cons, and no information as to its costs, while the head of the government announced early on that he would in any event do as he pleased, regardless of the results. This is not the kind of "democracy" that helps foster a democratic political culture.

The end result of these circumstances is that there is no consensus on the question of where Mexico is in its process of political development. Is it a democracy, or is it merely in transition toward becoming one? When did that transition begin and how will it end? There are questions about economic development as well. Basic issues that appeared to have been put to rest—whether the economy should remain open or return to protectionism, whether foreign investment is desirable or not, whether the government should reclaim a leading position in the economy—have once again surfaced. The recession in the United States and new political realities in places as different as Venezuela and Brazil—have added fuel to the fire and called into question the continuity of the economic policies of the past two decades.

What Is Missing and What Is Possible

While Mexican politics has undergone traumatic change, the lot of the average citizen has been transformed hardly at all. Politics in the old days meant closed-door negotiations in a smoke-filled room, whereas today's politics are out in the open. Beyond this, however, there is little difference. Dealings among politicians are no more transparent or less corrupt than they were, and accountability has not improved. If anything, the ability to enact policy has withered away due to the mismatch between executive and legislative power. Thus, the advances on the electoral front have not translated into gains for the citizenry. In this light, it is not surprising that many Mexicans are finding themselves disenchanted with their new democracy. Nothing suggests that this disenchantment will lead anywhere else, but it is a measure of the depth of the impasse. One of the key questions is whether a single political actor, such as the Supreme Court, can succeed in reshaping the political landscape and introduce a new institutional arrangement capable of delivering benefits directly to the average citizen, or whether the gridlock that characterizes Mexican politics today will continue.

The midterm elections in July 2003 proved not to be the major watershed that many expected. Even though the PRI won 223 seats (in a 500-seat chamber) and the PAN lost almost half of its representation, neither party ended up with an absolute majority. The latter notwithstanding, the voters sent a clear message: once in government, what matters are not promises, but delivering on them. The biggest loser in the elections was Fox, rather than the PAN. Whatever agenda Fox might have wanted to advance, the new political configuration puts much greater emphasis on negotiations with the PRI. It is the PRI that will determine the agenda for the remainder of Fox's term. Achieving such cooperation need not constitute an impossible task and, in fact, given the lack of concrete achievements over the past three years, the election results may prove to be the kick-start that Mexican politics needs. Most important, since all eyes will be fixed on the 2006 presidential elections, all parties, and above all the PRI, have an interest in showing that they can get things done.

The political process is extremely fluid at present. In the absence of rules, every actor in Mexican politics is attempting to strengthen itself through whatever means possible. One governor has gone so far as to stage his own personal demonstration (asking for more funds) in front of the presidential palace in Mexico City. The nature of the checks and balances that ultimately will emerge will determine the propensity for cooperation or paralysis among these various actors. And this, in turn, will depend on the vision, skills, and responsibility of key individuals, particularly the president and members of the Congress, over the next several months and years. Cooperation ebbs and flows depending on outside variables; in some instances, it depends on who has the upper hand at the moment among the various advisers inside the presidential palace; at others, it may be related to the latest polls in a minor state. Only when the costs of gridlock come to outweigh its benefits, as perceived by the political actors (some of whom hope to embarrass the president, for example), will political actors begin to negotiate in earnest. And that could take years.

There are several bills currently before the Congress under the heading of "Reform of the State" that represent attempts to restructure Mexico's institutions in order to cope with the new political realities. Most of these bills focus on old problems, such as trying to further weaken the presidency, but others address more pressing issues, such as reelection, the number of members of Congress and its composition (whether to maintain a mix of direct and proportional representation), and so on. It will take a long time to work through these bills and find solutions to the complexity that characterizes Mexican politics. But it is important to recall that, historically, Mexico has confronted its problems not through grand, visionary transformations, but rather through a series of incremental steps, often two forward and one backward, that do not appear dramatic but that get the job done.

The new political reality is undoubtedly complex, fluid, and uncertain. But it would have been unrealistic to expect otherwise. Given the circumstances of the political transition under way in Mexico for many years, the current uncertainty was the only realistic option. Voters seem to understand this fact and do not blame the president for gridlock. But much remains to be resolved. The political and economic environment has changed in ways that directly affect the citizenry—two examples are the economic stalemate and the standoff between Congress and the executive—but Mexicans have gained little power to deal with this new environment. Politicians bear a great responsibility to attempt to change that equation in the coming years.

Whatever the final outcome, the Mexico that emerged from the 2000 elections will never be the same. Although unruly, Mexican politics have now dispersed political power to such an extent that the likelihood of a return to old-style authoritarian excesses has virtually disappeared. In this, Mexicans have gained enormously. The process of building a democratic polity will likely be painful and complex. But it will never be as difficult as the uncertainty, insecurity, and abuse that were the traits of the past.

Mexico faces a quandary, but odds are it will resolve it reasonably well. The real question for the country's future is not whether it will successfully transform its political system, but whether this will happen in a timely fashion. While Mexicans see their politicians fight and accomplish little, the country's infrastructure, its educational and technological foundations, and virtually everything else needed to accelerate the pace of development remain stagnant. That's what really matters and nobody is doing anything about it.

Notes

1. Mathew Soberg Shugart and Stephan Haggard, "Institutions and Public Policy in Presidential Systems," in Stephan Haggard and Mathew D. McCubbins (eds.), *Presidents, Parliaments and Public Policy,* New York: Cambridge University Press, 2001, p. 80.

2. Presidencia de la República, *Segundo Informe de Gobierno, Anexo 2,* Mexico: Presidencia de la República, 2002.

2

Fox's Economic Agenda: An Incomplete Transition

Edna Jaime[1]

The reform of the Mexican economy has lost momentum. Evidence from the past three years shows that economic vitality is based on NAFTA-related exports and when these decline or fail to grow, so does the domestic economy. Further reform is needed to generate wealth and ensure that it is distributed more fairly. However, nearly twenty years after the first actions were implemented to open up the Mexican economy, the transition is still incomplete. Economic policy is contradictory, embodying both elements of reform and the legacy of the past. It seeks to foster competition, yet still protects sectors critical to modernization. It is committed to the creation of a consumer-based economy, but too often continues to serve producers and vested interests. It combines a liberal, market-oriented model with one reflective of Mexico's traditional corporatist state.[2] The failure to complete the economic reform agenda launched two decades ago has trapped Mexico in a costly state of limbo. The question is whether the Fox administration can pick up the reform agenda where it was abandoned and complete the transition.

During the 2000 election campaign, Vicente Fox appeared to be a promising candidate as far as economic issues were concerned. As a maverick from the opposition National Action Party (PAN), he was bound neither by the past nor by commitments to the vested interests of the old system. The expectations he raised, however, have yet to be fulfilled. These expectations were based, first, on his promotion of the idea of "change," which has been left largely undefined. They also arose from his generous promises of economic growth and his emphasis on education, health, and major investments in Mexico's poorest regions. Finally, expectations were furthered by discussion of structural reforms in the areas of tax policy and the electricity sector, among others, to which he appeared to be committed. In short, Vicente Fox promised to take up the unfinished reform agenda and see it to completion.

More than halfway through his six-year term, Fox has little to show for his efforts. There has been neither reform nor growth. The only achievements the government can point to are macroeconomic stability and the fact that it has resisted the temptation to use public spending as a temporary means of stimulating growth. Without reforms that promote competition and do away with monopolies and other vestiges of the protectionist past, the Mexican economy will be unable to achieve its full potential. Instead, a nation that has become increasingly dependent on its export sector must await an upturn in the U.S. economy. Having a strong export sector, however—even one that is regaining its dynamism—is no guarantee that the benefits of growth will be extended to the rest of the economy and to the population as a whole.

The president has lost the enthusiasm with which he began his term. He has failed to advance his economic agenda or project a clear sense of direction, while his hold on both his policy team and the population has weakened. The midterm elections in July 2003 were a major setback for the PAN, which lost 54 seats in the Chamber of Deputies, slipping from 205 to 151 of a total of 500 seats. The loss reflected the voters' disenchantment with the lack of results in all spheres, particularly the economy.

Without presidential leadership to promote the necessary reforms and a well-defined strategy to unite the population, the economic agenda of this administration will continue to drift, waiting for a verdict from legislative commissions or suffering attacks by its critics and those vested interests that benefit from the status quo. The divided Congress produced by the midterm elections, in which no party enjoys an absolute majority, will force the president to cope with the complexity of brokering agreements to advance his economic agenda. At the midpoint of his tenure, the question is no longer whether Fox will be able to give the reform process a final boost but whether he will be able even to offset the costs of Mexico's incomplete transition.

A Long Journey, but to Where?

Jesús Silva Herzog Márquez wrote in 1999 that "it sometimes seems that the transition has become the regime and that the road has turned into a permanent settlement."[3] This description of the political climate in Mexico prior to 2000 applies equally well to the current economic situation. The economic transition has reached a stalemate and the impetus of the initial reforms that opened up the borders to foreign competition, privatized countless public firms, and deregulated various economic sectors has been replaced by retreat.

Having said this, however, it is impossible to ignore the enormous changes that have taken place. The North American Free Trade Agreement (NAFTA), which more than doubled Mexico's exports to the United States, together with the number of Mexican firms that have become world leaders, is the best testimony to the progress the country has achieved. Nonetheless, the Mexican economy has not followed a path of sustained growth that would create opportunities for a rapidly growing population that requires incorporation into labor markets. Although it has managed to differentiate itself from other emerging markets, the Mexican economy is now, precisely because of its broader links to the world economy, more exposed than ever to the challenges posed by the international environment. These include the challenge of increasing productivity, coping with the knowledge and information revolution, and dealing with growing competition from countries such as China. If the Mexican economy fails to complete its process of transformation, it will risk economic stagnation or face a future with such limited growth that the nation will be unable to resolve many of its social problems.

Mexico's transition toward a market economy bears the stamp of the interests and circumstances that initially brought it about. The economic reforms of the 1980s and 1990s were undertaken grudgingly and against the wishes and instincts of the political leaders at the time. Reform came about only because a unique set of circumstances literally forced emergency measures to be adopted.

Even as Mexico experimented with different economic policies between the 1950s and the 1980s, one feature remained unchanged: the protection from outside competition that the government had offered domestic producers, a strategy known as import-substitution industrialization. For these twenty-five years, the economy experienced high growth rates, achieving rapid industrialization and urbanization and a significant expansion of the middle classes. In the 1950s and 1960s, this growth took place within an extremely stable environment, with orthodox monetary and fiscal policies. The government spent no more than it collected, meaning that public debt was also moderate, and this expenditure, oriented mainly toward infrastructure, had the effect of boosting the productivity of private investment. The 1970s and early 1980s, however, saw a rapid rise in expenditures (the tax deficit rose to 17 percent of GDP in 1982),[4] public debt (external debt grew from less than $2 billion to over $82 billion),[5] and oil production. The jettisoning of orthodox fiscal and monetary practices was soon felt in the form of currency devaluation, inflation, and above all, an enormous external debt, the servicing of which became impossible by 1982.

The eruption of the debt crisis that year showed that the import-substitution model was no longer valid and that, far from being strengthened by protection, Mexican firms had created inefficient processes, the costs of which were being paid by consumers. The problem was compounded by the fact that these firms were incapable of exporting to obtain foreign currency. This model had spawned various interests that, protected by the regulations restricting competition, enjoyed monopolistic profits. Mexico had developed what might be called a rent-seeking economy in which bureaucrats, through permits, restrictions, and subsidies, largely determined the way resources were allocated and how privileges (such as tax exemptions, subsidies, and import permits) were granted. This arrangement meshed perfectly with the structure and logic of the Mexican political system. The government was able to share economic privileges in return for the loyalty of organized groups and corporations within the ruling Institutional Revolutionary Party (PRI)—an exchange that benefited the party but hurt the country in terms of efficiency and competitiveness.

Major reforms began in 1985, largely due to the government's inability to restore growth using traditional mechanisms. In the midst of the debt crisis, the administration of Miguel de la Madrid (1982–1988) had struggled to restore fiscal and macroeconomic balance, but the situation remained extremely serious. Programs were implemented to stabilize the economy and reduce the deficit, all to no effect. The economy needed more than a program for economic stabilization, something the de la Madrid team was eventually forced to admit in view of its initial failure. Tentatively and somewhat unconvinced, the administration launched several important initiatives: it privatized some state-owned companies, negotiated Mexico's entry into the General Agreement on Tariffs and Trade (GATT), and allowed imports to enter the country, albeit with relatively high tariffs. These measures were an attempt to raise public income and force the country's productive sector to improve quality, raise productivity, and satisfy consumers. After decades of protectionism, these measures constituted a monumental change. The following years would see further reforms, all intended to achieve the same objectives.

In seeking to raise the growth rate, the governments of the 1980s and 1990s broke many of Mexico's deeply rooted principles of economic management. Their scope of action, however, was limited by an equally powerful objective that was responsible for many of the country's subsequent setbacks. Economic reform was bound by the central condition that it must not alter the traditional political structure of the PRI regime. In other words, the government could liberalize trade and encourage internal reform only so far as it did not affect the groups and vested interests closest to the party. These powerful interests included the unions of parastatal firms, such as the state oil company PEMEX and the electricity monopoly CFE, peasant organizations, and unions within the government bureaucracy itself, all of which served a key role in supporting the regime. The sources of power, control, and enrichment that were the essence of Mexican politics remained untouched, as did the corporatist structure of the PRI, while specific firms, especially those within the energy sector, remained protected. These limitations have severely hindered the effectiveness of reform, and the economic transition has been slow and painful as a result.

Mexican-Style *Perestroika*

Under Carlos Salinas's administration (1988–1994), Mexico quickened the pace of reform, improving public finances by reducing public expenditures, increasing tax collection, and controlling inflation; liberalizing trade; privatizing state-owned firms; granting autonomy to the central bank; and deregulating key sectors of the economy. Contradicting historical taboos, the Salinas government seemed prepared to modernize Mexico's productive structure and integrate it into the world economy.

▽ Most notably, the government eliminated barriers to all kinds of international trade, giving Mexico one of the most open economies in the world. In 1983, 100 percent of imported products were either prohibited or subject to some type of control, whereas by 1994, only 1.3 percent of imported goods continued to be subject to control (see Table 2.1). The Salinas government went even further by negotiating a free trade agreement with North America that opened the doors to the U.S. market for Mexican exports and to an unprecedented degree of competition for the national economy. Today, trade accounts for over 50 percent of Mexico's GDP, whereas in 1985 it contributed barely half this amount.[6]

These dramatic changes were possible because of the characteristics of the PRI and of the political system as a whole. The system gave the executive branch enormous power, enabling it to apply painful reforms designed to achieve economic stabilization, make severe cuts in public spending, and implement monetary policies that restricted liquidity, all without affecting political stability. In short, Carlos Salinas had the agenda, the instruments, and the power to undertake the process of

Table 2.1 Percentage of Products Controlled and Forbidden

	Import	Export
1983	100.0	13.9
1984	64.8	12.9
1985	10.4	8.4
1986	7.8	6.7
1987	3.9	6.8
1988	3.4	6.7
1989	2.6	7.1
1990	1.8	7.0
1991	1.7	6.6
1992	1.6	1.9
1993	1.6	1.9
1994	1.3	1.7
1995	0.7	1.7
1996	0.8	1.7
1997	0.8	1.4
1998	0.8	1.4
1999	0.8	1.4
2000	0.8	1.4
2001	0.8	1.4
2002[a]	0.8	0.5

Sources: Calculations based on data from the "Anexo del Sexto Informe de Gobierno" (Appendix to the 6th State of the Union Address), 1994, p. 148, and the "Anexo del Segundo Informe de Gobierno" (Appendix to the 2nd State of the Union Address), 2002, p. 283.

Note: a. Preliminary figures.

economic transformation. The stabilization policies, however, incurred steep social costs; during the period from 1987 to 1994, the real minimum salary lost over 40 percent of its value.[7]

The adjustment process to which the industrial sector was subjected by the shock of having to compete with imports was also painful. The process of industrial adjustment did not evolve in classic textbook fashion; it was not fluid and firms suffered innumerable setbacks. In very general terms, economic theory predicts that when an economy is opened to international trade flows it undergoes a process of specialization in which sectors with competitive advantages expand, while those that lack them contract. Trade liberalization has in fact led to the specialization of the Mexican productive apparatus, although the costs of this adjustment have been high. Mexico's greatest competitive advantage is the low cost of labor, which is why the *maquila* sector in the clothing and electronic-product assembly industries, among others, benefited and expanded significantly. Other examples include the automotive sector where intra-industry trade has created enormous opportunities for the

Mexican automobile parts industry. Conversely, the incipient electronics industry in Mexico has virtually disappeared, as have the textile and toy industries. These industries thrived under protectionism, but once it was abolished, they gradually lost their relative share of the manufacturing product. The most striking fact, however, is that most small and medium-sized industry continues to depend entirely on the internal market (which has been depressed) because of its inability to establish links with the export sector. This explains why the benefits of free trade have been so limited and why the export-linked growth of the 1990s failed to help the bulk of the population.

It is difficult to imagine such a process of macroeconomic stabilization and microeconomic adjustment occurring under current political conditions. The vertical structure of political control and decisionmaking that characterized the political system in the late 1980s allowed the reforms to advance virtually without interruption provided they did not harm the political or electoral base of the PRI. The Economic Solidarity Pact (1987–1996), the name given to the heterodox program of economic stabilization described above, is an excellent example of the effectiveness of Mexico's corporatist arrangements. The leaders of worker, peasant, business, and government organizations agreed to curb wage demands and price increases for goods and services, including those provided by the government, in order to coordinate the expectations of economic actors and eliminate the inertial component of inflation. These leaders were then able to impose the terms of the agreement on other members of their organizations, often in exchange for a particular benefit, but also through the threat of punishment or exclusion. The pact proved successful because the underlying control mechanisms were effective.

These control mechanisms, however, were eroded as economic reform advanced. To the extent that the government privatized state firms, deregulated economic sectors, and gradually allowed the market to assign resources, the mechanisms and resources underpinning the traditional system of control began to disappear. There were fewer privileges and fewer sources of corruption to share. Within the logic of import-substitution industrialization, a business's profits or income were dependent on bureaucracies. These determined which business would have the benefit of an import permit, in the case of foreign trade, for example, or the regulations that would govern a particular economic activity. High entry barriers were often imposed on new competitors in sectors as diverse as cargo transport and banking, or tax exemptions were granted with no apparent justification. Bureaucracies enjoyed an enormous amount of discretionary power, which gave rise to corruption. Trade liberalization, economic deregulation, and privatization gradually undermined the power of the bureaucracies, reducing the opportunity for such abuses.

Despite the reformist nature of Carlos Salinas's administration, its agenda for economic change was always limited. Vital sectors of the economy were shielded from the reforms that shook the rest of the productive structure. In this respect, reform was partial; the logic of competition was imposed on the manufacturing sector, while the logic of protectionism prevailed in other major sectors, such as energy, telecommunications, and finance.

After the midterm elections of 1991, in which Salinas's leadership was confirmed after the highly dubious election that he won in 1988, the president could have taken a definitive step toward the transformation of the national economy. Doing so, however, would have implied a dismantling of the traditional political system without providing an alternative to ensure political stability and garner sufficient support for the PRI in the upcoming presidential elections.[8] Consequently, Mexico's corporatist structures were left intact and specific sectors and firms continued to be granted levels of protection that even now restrict the rest of the economy's capacity for success. Although daring, Salinas's reforms essentially built on the past, rather than doing away with it.

Even so, the Salinas legacy in economic matters should not be underestimated. The reforms of this period lent vitality and greater institutional support to the economy. The most important steps were NAFTA and the legal reforms that granted autonomy to the central bank. The trade agreement and the exports associated with it have become the main source of growth for the Mexican economy, while central bank autonomy is now a pillar of macroeconomic stability. Central bank policies, the main aim of which is to control inflation, have gradually moved away from politics; in other words, they are no longer driven by the needs of the incumbent president, which makes them more predictable and credible.

Salinas embarked on an ambitious process of economic transformation that he failed to complete. Since then, the reform agenda has searched for a leader and the political agreements needed to promote it. One or the other has always been missing. In this respect, the outlook for advancing the agenda of pending structural reforms and completing this complex transition is less than promising.

Zedillo and the Administration of a Crisis

In his inaugural address, Ernesto Zedillo (1994–2000) scarcely referred to economic issues. His agenda would be dominated by politics: if Carlos Salinas had promoted *perestroika,* Zedillo would advance *glasnost.*

He mentioned the ambitious legal reform he intended to undertake, together with the need for a "definitive" electoral reform that would ensure transparency and fairness during electoral processes, which had always been marred by accusations of fraud. The focus of the address turned out to be ironic, since the Zedillo administration soon found itself concerned with a single issue: restoring stability in the aftermath of the economic crisis that erupted at the beginning of his administration.

In Mexico, the notion of economic crisis is associated with currency devaluation, but also with the end of every *sexenio*. Since 1976, each change of government has almost religiously been accompanied by a currency devaluation, followed by economic contraction and inflation.[9] This pattern is by no means a coincidence. On the eve of an election, economic policy was traditionally placed at the service of politics, which often entailed an increase in public spending to encourage growth, leading in turn to a crisis in the balance of payments and a subsequent adjustment of the exchange rate. Nineteen ninety-four, the year Salinas handed over power to his successor, was no exception. Despite reform, trade liberalization, NAFTA, and all the credibility on economic matters the president had built up throughout his administration. Mexico was fated to endure yet another crisis. However, 1994 was also unlike any other year.

In January, the very day NAFTA came into being, an Indian rebellion took the government by surprise. The Zapatistas launched a movement that demanded Salinas's resignation and opposed free trade. A few months later, political violence—absent from national life for over half a century—claimed the lives first of the PRI's then-presidential candidate, Luis Donaldo Colosio, and then its secretary general, José Francisco Ruiz Massieu. The volatile political situation and more attractive financial returns in the United States triggered a flight of capital that was contained at various points using a range of financial instruments. These instruments, however, far from reducing the vulnerability of the Mexican economy, actually increased it, as explained below.

The Mexican economy's Achilles' heel was the large deficit in its current account (nearly 7 percent of the GDP), a figure that caused little concern at the time because the country was still able to attract foreign investment on this scale. It was a deficit that could easily be financed, or so those responsible for economic policy argued. The investments that flowed into Mexico were mainly liquid, portfolio investments that would remain in the country as long as economic policy was credible and Mexican markets offered safe returns. In 1994, neither of these assumptions held true. Capital flight and the resulting loss of reserves led to the decision made under Zedillo to modify the exchange rate policy, with devastating results for the Mexican economy.

Since 1987, a fixed exchange rate had been adopted as a nominal anchor for reducing the likelihood of inflation. The exchange rate could slide only within a band whose floor and ceiling had been set by the aforementioned Economic Solidarity Pact. The guarantee of exchange rate stability that this scheme offered made it even more attractive for foreigners to invest in a country that was regarded as the emerging economy of the moment. Provided investment flows were steady, things ran smoothly. With a credible economic policy, money would continue to flow in from abroad, financing the growing consumption of imported goods. The succession of events in 1994 destroyed these conditions and called for a change of strategy. Politics continued to drive economic decisions in 1994. On this occasion, as so often in the past, political criteria determined economic policy. This explains why the proximity of the 1994 presidential elections led to a change in economic policy designed to stimulate internal demand and therefore growth. Regardless of the enormous transformation that the Mexican economy had undergone, this criterion remained constant.

In the months leading up to the 1994 presidential elections, the government began to implement an expansionist policy, both fiscal and monetary, to jump-start the economy and give the PRI an advantage in the upcoming electoral contest.[10] The most advisable course at the time was to continue with the restrictive fiscal and monetary policy of previous months and modify the exchange rate system. A politically unpopular devaluation was out of the question, given the proximity of the elections. A fixed exchange rate policy, such as the one the government had implemented since 1987, could only be maintained if it were accompanied by strict fiscal discipline and a monetary policy focused on inflation control. These two conditions were relaxed a few months before the election.

In order to halt the flow of capital, the government designed a financial instrument known as the *tesobono,* a federal government bond that, although denominated in pesos, offered a guaranteed exchange rate into U.S. dollars at the maturity date. *Tesobonos* achieved their objective of neutralizing exchange risk for investors and reducing capital flight, but they left the government with an enormous short-term debt and forced it to assume the exchange risk. Months later, the scope of the problem became evident.

This was the situation bequeathed to Ernesto Zedillo when he assumed the presidency on December 1, 1994. The economy clearly required corrective measures to stop capital flight and restore confidence. However, neither the president's inaugural address nor the administration's key economic document accompanying the annual budget proposal to Congress even mentioned the problem. Investors' trust dwindled while capital flight continued unabated. Devaluation became inevitable.

Days after assuming the presidency, the Zedillo administration announced that the currency band within which the Mexican peso floated would be expanded. The modification of the monetary regime and the way it was carried out destroyed the government's credibility and triggered a massive devaluation and renewed capital flight, making it extremely difficult for the Mexican government to fulfill its short-term financial commitments, most of which were payable in foreign currency (namely *tesobonos*).

Zedillo's government was now accused of juggling its international reserves figures, manipulating information to suit the audience (using one set of figures abroad and another for domestic consumption), and lacking a plan to deal with the crisis—in short, undertaking economic policy measures that would minimize the costs of an imminent crisis. All this eroded the credibility that the Mexican government had built up in previous years. During his term, Zedillo embarked on the task of restoring this credibility, which he eventually succeeded in doing. In the process, however, he neglected what should have been his administration's economic agenda: the culmination of the transformation of the Mexican economy. What was needed, among other things, was to continue with the structural reforms still pending, particularly in the energy sector, but above all to create the conditions that would enable markets to operate efficiently. Just as foreign trade had been liberalized, there was a need to liberalize internal competition in sectors as diverse as telecommunications and finance. It was also necessary to establish an institutional environment conducive to market efficiency, including pro-competitive regulations in all sectors and an efficient, effective legal system that would protect property rights and enforce contracts.

Far from implementing a reform agenda, Zedillo's administration had to cope not only with the collapse of the exchange rate and accompanying capital flight, but also with the consequences of a financial system privatization that was badly conceived and even more poorly implemented. Banks, after being privatized in the early 1990s, had been offered incentives that encouraged them to take excessive risks and make poor lending decisions within the framework of universal insurance for deposits and the virtual lack of a supervising body. The 1994 financial crisis caused most of these credits to move into default, which, in turn, threatened to create a system-wide emergency.[11]

The economic aid package offered to the Mexican government by the United States, the International Monetary Fund, and the international financial community, as well as a series of late but effective measures taken by the Mexican government,[12] facilitated a relatively swift recovery. The crisis revealed that the transformation of the economy had been incomplete—political criteria still determined economic decisions—but the rapid recovery showed the other side of the coin: the Mexican economy had changed enough to be able to rely on its export sector as a source of dynamism.

Structural reforms were sidelined as the government struggled to stay ahead of the crisis. The government successfully implemented emergency reforms, such as a measure raising the value-added tax (VAT) from 10 percent to 15 percent to offset the drop in public income due to the decline of economic activity, and another involving pensions.[13] It was, however, unable to carry out other reforms that, once the emergency was over, would prove to be crucial to the country's future success.

In retrospect, it seems obvious that the administration believed that its legislative majority would remain intact following the 1997 midterm election. It was in this election, however, that the PRI lost its historic majority for the first time in seventy years. This marked a fundamental change in the conditions that had until then permitted legal and even constitutional changes in economic matters. But even without this institutional obstacle, Zedillo's economic agenda could never have been described as ambitious. One example is the electricity sector, which was showing signs of its own financial crisis. It had been clear for some time that public resources could not possibly provide the investment required for the electricity sector to be able to satisfy constantly growing demand. The government's response was a reform bill introduced late in the day. The attempt to eliminate the restriction on private investment in the sector and facilitate the privatization of the assets of the public firms that provide electricity service revealed another problem: resistance to the reforms came from within the party's own ranks. With the loss of the PRI's political monopoly, the president had lost the mechanisms through which he could impose discipline.[14] Excessive concentration of power in the presidency had given way to a weakened executive, further restricted by a Congress lacking a majority. Coupled with this was an obvious lack of skill and political cooperation on the part of the president for advancing his economic agenda, however limited it may have been. As a result of the privatization of state-owned firms, the elimination of entry barriers to various economic activities, and the government's withdrawal from economic activity, the executive branch no longer had its traditional sources of privilege, profits, and corruption to dispense. Economic reform and political change gradually undermined the presidency, turning it into a restricted and weakened office vis-à-vis other public powers and vested interests. The PRI apparatus and its innumerable control mechanisms were no longer available to offer support for an economic transition.

In spite of these setbacks, a number of extremely important decisions were made during Zedillo's term. Some aspects of the political project that Zedillo proposed in his inaugural address were advanced relatively successfully. In late 1994, a constitutional reform granted the Mexican Supreme Court of Justice new powers and turned it into a constitutional court with mechanisms for the nomination, replacement, and removal of magistrates—powers that ensure the autonomy of this collegiate body. In the traditional political system, the Supreme Court had always been subordinated to the executive branch and lacked the powers to review electoral issues and the constitutionality of laws. Individuals' political and civil rights had also been completely unprotected. The final arbiter was always the executive branch, which resolved disputes between the branches, levels of government, and even among individuals. Through the reform of the constitution, Zedillo transferred this role to the most important tribunal in the country, with important economic repercussions.[15] In the Supreme Court of Justice, the executive branch now has a counterweight that limits its room for maneuver in economic matters. Likewise, through an electoral reform enacted in 1996, the government transferred the role of organizing and supervising elections to an autonomous body. The main source of electoral manipulation was thereby eliminated. Vicente Fox's triumph at the polls in 2000 would have been impossible without this significant change in electoral processes.

Unlike proposed reforms that directly challenged vested interests, such as the electricity sector bill that would impinge on trade union privileges, these two reforms involved the president renouncing the extraconstitutional powers and prerogatives that had long given the office enormous power. Electoral reform was agreed on by the main political forces and undoubtedly signified enormous progress in the country's democratization.

The democratization Zedillo wished to promote yielded fruit, but it also hampered the decisionmaking process on economic issues. The executive branch continues to have the power to define economic strategy and pursue specific policies, but structural reforms like the opening of certain sectors to private investment require confrontation with vested interests intent on defending their prerogatives, as well as a reckoning with the diverse political forces now represented in Congress. Economic reform no longer depends on the decision of a single office or branch of government. It will have to proceed through negotiations and, as a result, future reforms are likely to be incremental. Executive leadership is critical in such a context, especially because Mexico's institutional framework has not adapted to these new realities of power. For his part, Zedillo, obsessed with the goal of stability, was either unwilling or unable to advance the economic reform agenda.

In political terms, any attempt at future economic reform will have to overcome the resistance not only of vested interests but also of public opinion. Surveys conducted on key aspects of economic reform have shown that the public is divided. On specific issues, such as opening up the electricity or petroleum sectors, the majority of Mexicans continue to defend the status quo, believing that state control of these strategic sectors is crucial for protecting national sovereignty.

Economic reform has already changed the country's productive structure, the direction of the government's development policy and agenda, and Mexico's exposure to the international environment. Efforts by political leaders to communicate to citizens the need for continued reform is crucial, especially since these changes have failed to translate into a source of greater well-being for most Mexicans. This is the great paradox: reforms need popular support to be able to advance, yet they are intrinsically unpopular because they have failed to benefit people's pockets. The advantages of reforms have been concentrated in certain regions (primarily the north and center of the country) and sectors (mainly the manufacturing and *maquila* sectors). They have not benefitted Mexican employees and businesses equally, nor have they helped either group as consumers. Reforms have earned themselves a bad reputation, and no one in government is apparently willing to vindicate their objectives or undeniable achievements.

The Current Economic Problem

Economies throughout the world are facing a changing environment to which they must adapt. The problems of the Mexican economy, however, will involve making fundamental changes rather than peripheral adjustments. Mexico will have to expand its process of reform until it reaches the microeconomic level, which affects decisions concerning investment, innovation, and productivity.

One of the challenges that must be overcome is that Mexican firms and consumers pay more for services than their counterparts in other countries. Thus, Mexican firms start off at a disadvantage in the face of global competition. Tables 2.2 and 2.3 show a central irony of the

Table 2.2 Costs in the Energy Sector

	Electricity		Fuel	
	Residential electricity in dollars per kWh	Industrial electricity in dollars per kWh	Commercial diesel in dollars per liter	Regular unleaded gasoline in dollars per liter
OECD average	—	—	.528	.484
Mexico	.075	.053	.439	.584
United States	.085	.050	.371	.386
Canada	—	—	.445	.455
Argentina	.086	.069	.561	.917
Colombia	.064	.042	.249	.367
Costa Rica	.065	.076	.424	.583

Source: Energy Prices and Taxes, 2nd Quarter 2003, International Energy Agency, Data for 2001.

Table 2.3 Telecommunications Costs

	International Calls[a]	Residential Phone[b]	Business Phone[c]	Mobile Phone[d]	Internet[e]
OECD average	1.28	488.13	1074.96	n.a.	36.31
Mexico	3.73	747.97	2189.03	227.96	32.90
United States	.97	568.92	1148.65	152.46	33.58
Canada	.92	381.96	819.15	135.71	25.34

Source: Communications Outlook 2003, OECD.
Notes: 2002 data in U.S. dollars.
a. Average call charge for one single call, weighted by traffic.
b. OECD basket of residential telephone charges (includes international calls and calls to mobile networks).
c. OECD basket of business telephone charges (includes international calls and calls to mobile networks).
d. OECD basket of low-user mobile telephone charges.
e. OECD internet basket for twenty hours.

country's economic transition: one of the world's most open economies has some of the world's most closed domestic sectors. (In addition to the protected energy, petrochemicals, and telecommunications industries mentioned above, airlines, cement and the financial sector are subject to oligopolistic structures.)

The cost of electricity in Mexico is similar to that of other countries with which Mexican products compete. This rate, however, had a government subsidy of over 40 percent in 2002, the cost of which is exacted from other sources. Subsidies are often paid for by higher tax rates, for example. Rates for telecommunication services are much higher in Mexico than in other Organization for Economic Cooperation and Development (OECD) countries and even in other Latin American countries. The list goes on, and includes airfares, highway tolls, and the cost of capital, which is twice as high in Mexico as it is among the country's main trading partners.

The reason for this is quite simple: these are sectors that face no competition; hence, they have no incentives to increase productivity and efficiency by innovating or implementing technological changes or reducing the price of the product or service paid for by the end user. This result is largely unaffected by the public or private nature of ownership. Private monopolies such as Telmex or public ones such as PEMEX and CFE place an enormous burden on the economy as a whole and reduce the competitive potential of the rest of Mexican industry. Firms traditionally have offset the costs of the environment (higher rates for electricity, telecommunications, transport, and various other services) through the price of labor, although this has lost its attractiveness in comparative terms—average salaries in China are a fraction of what they are now in Mexico. As a result, firms operating in Mexico are becoming less competitive. There are no longer many alternatives. For foreign-owned entities, the best option is to emigrate, as many large, transnational companies are doing, while for the majority of Mexican firms the choice is to shut down or struggle to survive.

Although the prevailing view in many circles is that the lack of competition does not make much difference, proof of the opposite is overwhelming. If one observes the behavior of firms such as PEMEX and CFE in comparison with similar companies in other countries, the results are revealing. Firms like these are inefficient precisely because they do not have to deal with competition, nor does the regulatory framework provide them with the right incentives. These companies also support unions with enormous prerogatives, including salaries and benefits far above the national average; create uncertainty about the supply of services because there has been little investment in recent years; and make the rest of the economy pay for their inefficiency and unreliability. These are not marginal sectors, but rather industries that are central to all productive activity. And, as Table 2.4 shows, the productivity of Mexican workers in the electricity, petroleum, and telecommunications sectors is among the lowest of OECD members.

Worker productivity has no correlation with the actual power of the trade unions of the state-owned firms in question. After the PRI's failure to win the presidential elections in 2000, these unions lost their links

Table 2.4 Labor Productivity in the Energy and Telecommunications Sectors

	Electricity	Petroleum	Telecommunications
	Added value per worker (in dollars)		Income per worker (in dollars)
United States	249,826	232,060	228,132
Spain	174,606	267,410	147,875
Netherlands	156,509	233,790	252,373
United Kingdom	200,584	108,183	259,053
Mexico	33,611	39,915	139,309

Sources: The figures for electricity and petroleum were compiled by CIDAC using data from OECD, *Cuentas Nacionales de Países de la OCDE*, vol. 2, OECD, 2002. Since there are no specific figures on worker productivity, the average added value per worker was calculated. Data were used from the electricity, gas, and water supply industries and the coke manufacturing, refined petroleum products, and nuclear energy industries. Figures correspond to 1999, with the exception of Spain, for which data for 1997 were used. The telecommunications data were obtained from OECD, *Communications Outlook 2001*, Table 9.7.

to the party and the president. However, they did not lose their enormous influence. Monopolistic firms continue to dominate strategic sectors, and the mere threat of strikes makes the economy as a whole tremble. The corporatist pillars of the system, which at one time were essential to stabilizing the economy and producing economic growth, are now a disruptive element, not only because of their opposition to any reform, but also because of the privileged conditions they preserve for themselves.

These are but the most visible examples of the paradox of the Mexican economy and its incomplete transition. In addition to the difficulties governments have had in completing the agenda of structural reform, they have also failed to create the most basic public goods, such as legal security and the protection of property rights. Lawsuits are uncertain, lengthy, and costly, which is one reason why the banking sector has not channeled resources into the productive sector. (For example, the legal process of enforcing a banking guarantee in Mexico can take years, as opposed to a few months in the United States.) Investment in infrastructure is extremely limited (86 percent of public expenditure goes toward current spending, and only 14 percent for investment),[16] while levels of educational achievement are extremely low.[17] In short, the government has proven itself incapable of establishing clear rules of the game; regulations that encourage competition; or institutions that facilitate trade, create certainty and trust, and allow for the process

**Figure 2.1 Manufacturing Sector Productivity
(annual percentage change)**

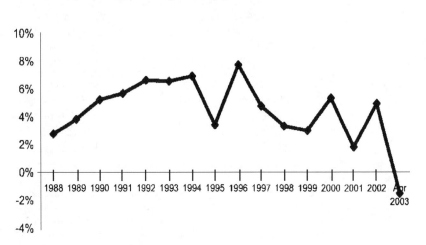

Source: CIDAC, based on information from Banco de México.

of "creative destruction" vital to any market economy.[18] The consequences are obvious: the Mexican economy is becoming less productive
and, in today's world, that means losing opportunities to develop (see
Figure 2.1).

The Mexican Rural Sector:
Stagnation and the Status Quo[19]

In the countryside, as in the rest of the economy, major reforms began
to be carried out, but they were never completed. During his administration, Carlos Salinas de Gortari attempted to implement a series of
institutional reforms aimed at redefining property rights in the rural sector. He had concluded, quite rightly, that the rural problem, characterized by a lack of capitalization as well as low profitability and productivity of agricultural activities, was due to problems with the definition
of property rights, weak mechanisms for protecting them, and enormous
legal uncertainty arising from these issues.

Over seventy years of land distribution had done away with the
notion of private property and had also hindered efficiency. Expropriation

was a very real threat during the years when land was distributed. Under the agrarian laws of the time, a person affected by expropriation was not entitled to go to court to defend his property. One effect of the uncertainty caused by the lack of protection of property rights in the country was a systematic reduction in investment. There was no incentive to invest in one's land if it was liable to be expropriated. But land distribution also created another distortion. Imposing limits on the size of private holdings and dividing up the land that was distributed into increasingly small plots created production units of an economically inefficient scale (60 percent of peasants cultivate fewer than five hectares[20]). Although there have always been successful commercial farmers who have managed to get around government prohibitions, particularly in the north, the Mexican countryside is characterized by subsistence farming, with plots of land no larger than twenty hectares.

The rural problem was also due to a form of land ownership known as the *ejido*.[21] Under this system, farm workers were entitled to use, but not to own, the land they lived on and cultivated. Without property deeds, peasants were unable to gain access to commercial banking credits. Their avenues for financing were therefore confined to the government development bank, which was dominated by political interests. At the time of the 1992 reform, *ejidos* accounted for 50 percent of national territory.

After seventy years, Carlos Salinas put an end to the distribution of agricultural land, something his predecessors had not dared to do.[22] He also allowed *ejido* peasants to change their form of land ownership to private property if they so wished. Other measures included lifting the restrictions prohibiting the participation of trading concerns in the countryside and granting *ejidos* the right to free association and to lease or sell their lands. The reforms also established the creation of agrarian courts to settle land disputes. Until then, agrarian disputes had been resolved by the president, through the Agrarian Reform Secretariat. The aim of these reforms was to establish the conditions for introducing market mechanisms in the countryside, eliminating legal insecurity, and providing for greater flows of capital into the rural sector.

The redefinition of property rights in the rural environment was to serve as the touchstone for its transformation. More than ten years later, the countryside has shown some signs of modernization. The process of defining property rights continues to advance, and certain parts of the country, particularly in the north, have converted their crops into more competitive, stable commodities,[23] taking advantage of access to the

U.S. market provided by NAFTA.[24] Nevertheless, agricultural activities are still so unprofitable that they fail to attract investment. As in the rest of the economy, efforts at reform were suspended by the 1994–1995 crisis and subsequently abandoned.

The profitability of the agricultural sector hinges on the availability of timely supplies at competitive prices, to which Mexican producers do not have access. Rural producers experience severe difficulties in obtaining sufficient, high-quality, competitively priced inputs, such as seeds, fertilizers, electricity, machinery, and credit. The protectionism that prevailed for decades in the Mexican economy meant that, given the lack of competition, the providers of supplies for farming activity— government firms such as Fertilizantes Mexicanos (Fertimex) and Productora Nacional de Semillas—lacked incentives either to lower the price of their products or to make their distribution and supply mechanisms more efficient. These firms were privatized, but no competitive markets emerged to replace them. Within the framework of trade liberalization, the authorities calculated that access to supplies from abroad would suffice to create competition in the domestic market. But both government and producers were taken unaware by the 1994–1995 crisis, which shelved the initiative. The economic crisis, together with devaluation, made importing supplies for agricultural activities prohibitively expensive.

Although increased importation of farm supplies has gradually mitigated the problem of access, the persistently high costs of products or services supplied by government monopolies (such as the price of electricity, which rose 77 percent in real terms between 1990 and 2001, and 56 percent between 1994 and 2001) have more than offset the advantages associated with lower-cost imported products.

Financing for the rural sector also fell drastically after the 1994–1995 crisis. As Figure 2.2 shows, private financing reached record levels in 1994, exceeding the amount assigned by the government through its development bank. While the express purpose of the 1992 reform was to encourage private individuals to participate in the capitalization of the countryside, the crisis and ensuing rise in overdue commercial credits reduced the amounts of financing available in real terms. Commercial banks cut their share of credit to the agricultural sector, since it was perceived as being too risky. In fact, since the contraction experienced by the commercial banking sector between 1991 and 1995, commercial banks have never returned to their previous patterns of granting credit. Because agricultural activities are riskier than either manufacturing activities or consumer loans, commercial credit in the sector is unlikely to revive, particularly when over half the land in Mexico is

**Figure 2.2 Real Credit Given to the Farming Sector
(millions of 1994 pesos)**

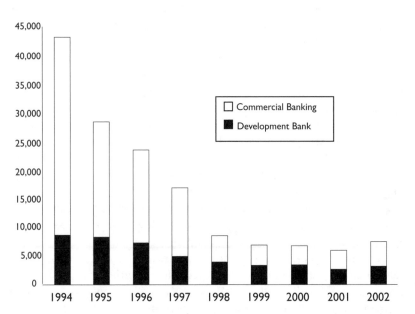

Source: Figure based on the statistical appendix of the Segundo Informe de Gobierno de la Administración Federal, 2000–2006.

Note: These amounts do not include expired portfolios—in other words, they include only the amounts effectively given to producers (usually called "fresh credit").

used for seasonal farming—meaning that it has no irrigation infrastructure, making productivity completely dependent on the weather. At the same time, the amount of credit channeled through the national development bank is insufficient. Banco de Crédito Rural (Banrural), the development bank for the countryside, was liquidated in early 2003 because of its inefficiency and copious losses. Banrural operated more as a political instrument than a financial institution. An extremely low percentage of the credits it granted were recovered, and these in any case were given to politically advantageous clients rather than to those peasants and farmers ineligible for commercial bank credit that should have been its target group. The political logic that governed the institution was revealed when the funds granted by Banrural were shown to increase during each electoral period.

Once an agricultural producer has dealt with production costs, he then has to cope with those associated with transport, storage, and the sale of his products. Transport costs are high, the quality of highway infrastructure is poor, and there is a widespread lack of public safety on the roads. In forestry production, transport accounts for 70 percent of costs, due to the infrequent maintenance of both trucks and highway infrastructure and the high cost of toll roads.[25] Airports, highways, bridges, and railroads have increased their rates, which also negatively affects producers.

In addition to the above, most agricultural producers face enormous difficulties in selling their products. Most producers are concentrated in tiny, scattered settlements, with very small harvests and no infrastructure to link them to consumer centers. This gives rise to a host of intermediaries who, given the high cost of alternatives, have great leverage and absorb much of the producers' profit margins. At other times, when the producer or group of producers assumes the cost of storing and transporting products, taking them to be sold at regional distribution and sales centers, they confront an oligopolistic structure of very few buyers who collude to set extremely low prices. These virtual monopsonies (where there is only one buyer of the item sold) are tolerated because of the enormous amount of power they wield through their control of the food supplies of Mexico's major cities. No government has ever dared challenge them and, although government programs have been implemented to commercialize farm products, the efforts have been extremely bureaucratic and often plagued by corruption.

These distortions in the agricultural product market considerably reduce the profitability of the sector. The successful cases of agricultural production in Mexico have involved the evasion of internal supply constraints and product markets plagued by dysfunction and anomalies. To mention just one example, the financing of crop conversion is covered by the partners' own capital or by seeking credit abroad at lower rates, since credit in Mexico is either inaccessible or too expensive (a Mexican producer has to pay three times more interest than his counterparts in the United States or Canada).

The economic transition in the countryside was incipient but deep. Putting an end to agrarian distribution, promoting the regularization of plots of land whose ownership was in dispute, and creating the possibility of turning those with shares in common holdings into the owners of their land clearly eliminated one of the most pernicious causes of rural backwardness. The restructuring of the countryside, however, required many more reforms that were never carried out. A decade after having negotiated NAFTA, the countryside remains paralyzed. It is hardly a coincidence that it is also the place where the country's extreme poverty is concentrated (80 percent of families in the countryside are poor).

For many years, the Mexican countryside constituted a source of unconditional support for the PRI regime and a supply of cheap votes obtained by mobilizing the rural population with the promise of land, credit that would never materialize, and supplies at subsidized prices. Government actions in the Mexican countryside followed the logic of political control, always sidestepping its political costs. The land distribution system lasted for a period of seventy-five years, a fact that can be understood only by recognizing that the promise of land was used to guarantee support for the regime. This period also saw the reduction of the productive potential of this economic sector.

Unfortunately, although the institutional reforms undertaken by the Salinas administration in the countryside changed this political logic, they fell short of their objectives. The distortions in markets, together with the lack of supply and distribution mechanisms, are still facts of life. The concept of choice does not exist for farm workers in rural settings. As long as markets in the countryside continue to operate under these conditions, farm workers will continue to be controlled by intermediaries and local moneylenders. They will also remain subject to clientelistic practices in which access to supplies, credit, or a distribution channel is contingent on political support or mobilization in favor of a particular cause. In the past, these practices benefited the PRI, and they now contribute to the political capital of leaders or intermediaries who offer their services to the highest bidder. In the 2000 election, the rural vote could not be mobilized as effectively as it had been in the past. This is another of the factors that explain the PRI's defeat at the polls that year.

Although the notion of economic reform refers far more often to the manufacturing, service, or financial sectors of the economy than to the more traditional activities of the primary sector, it is precisely here that an agenda for change is most urgently needed. Only through such an agenda will the profitability and productivity of the Mexican countryside increase.

Vicente Fox: A Time for Reduced Expectations?

These are some of the challenges facing Vicente Fox's administration in economic affairs. The success of the president's goals cannot be measured only by growth in the GDP or the level of exports, but must also be judged by his capacity to transform and give direction to the Mexican economy. In short, will the current president be able to take up the agenda of economic reforms that was abandoned and without which the Mexican economy will be unlikely to benefit the majority of the population?

During the campaign, Vicente Fox's economic agenda was vague. He promised 7 percent growth, greater expenditure on health and education, infrastructure for the most backward states in the country, microcredits, and support for small businesses—in other words, nothing that would commit him too heavily or alienate possible allies. His triumph in the 2000 presidential election was not based on a well-defined economic agenda, but on the promise of change that accompanied each of his declarations.

Once he assumed the presidency, Fox drew up an agenda of structural reforms (i.e., those affecting the tax, labor, telecommunications, and energy regimes) as part of his economic project. The problem is that his economic agenda rested on reforms whose approval depended entirely on Congress, where the numbers in the legislature did not give his party a majority. The 2003 midterm elections have put him at an even greater disadvantage, with the PAN holding just 153 out of a possible 500 seats in the Chamber of Deputies. Although it is essential to deal with the issue of structural reform, since it ultimately determines the economy's capacity to grow, Fox overlooked the many aspects of economic policy that can be transformed from within the confines of the executive branch. These include strengthened mechanisms for regulating and promoting competition, simplified paperwork and procedures for starting a business, design schemes to enable private investors to participate in the construction or maintenance of infrastructure, and measures to deal with the problem of safety in the streets and low educational standards. None of these issues has been effectively tackled. Several programs were created in the fields of education, the environment, the countryside, and health, but they have failed to attack the underlying problems. Wherever there are vested interests, the government has withdrawn. One example is education, where the initiatives of the current administration (such as the creation of an Institute for Educational Evaluation), although commendable, have stopped short of modifying the status of the powerful teachers' union that controls resources, tenure, and salaries without taking merit, training, or quality into account. Another example is the rural sector, where a national agreement signed in March 2003 is simply a continuation of previous policies. The agreement provides abundant resources and subsidies that, far from solving existing structural problems (such as distortions in the supply market, inappropriate distribution channels, and lack of credit), have actually maintained their status quo.

In contrast, the structural reforms proposed by the executive branch challenge the status quo and affect powerful interests, which is precisely why they are so difficult to implement. The bill proposed by the executive branch to reform the electricity sector is paradigmatic in this respect. In it, the administration suggests opening up the sector to private investment, a move that implies a loss of monopoly power and associated union prerogatives by the two parastatal firms in the sector, the Federal Electricity Commission and Luz y Fuerza del Centro. The triumph of these interests over the executive branch was furthered by uninformed public opinion, which fails to grasp the need for reforms; deeply rooted ideas of sovereignty as synonymous with public ownership of firms in strategic sectors; an ideologically divided political class that lacks consensus on the best means of revitalizing the economy; a legislature, at least during the first three years of Fox's term, with a powerful desire for revenge and every interest in seeing the president fail; and an executive branch that has lost its power to lead. All these forces underscore the fact that Vicente Fox inherited a very different presidency from that of his predecessors—one that lacks both a majority in the legislative branch and the political instruments that the old political system gave its presidents.

The Mexican economy is clearly not going to collapse in the short term, but without reforms, conditions in the productive sector will continue to deteriorate. The macroeconomic situation is stable because of the determination shown by this administration in its handling of macroeconomic issues. The administration has maintained strict fiscal control and a monetary policy designed to reduce inflation in order to be able to converge with Mexico's trading partners in this respect. Stability is undoubtedly a precondition for everything else, but it is not enough. Even this stability will be at risk if nothing is done. The government must cope with an enormous contingent debt resulting from, among other things, the rescue of the banks orchestrated during the Zedillo administration and the collapse of the state workers' pension scheme. Fiscal balance is also subject to growing pressure from subnational governments. The tax collection and expenditure structure creates perverse incentives, in that the federation collects revenues while subnational governments spend them with no control or accountability mechanisms.

Vicente Fox's first defeat in the legislative branch was precisely in the area of taxes. The most salient aspect of his tax initiative, presented shortly after taking office, proposed the standardization of the VAT rate to 15 percent. The VAT currently carries different rates and exemptions for certain products, such as food and medicine. This scheme encouraged tax evasion and made administration extremely difficult. The reform was necessary in that it would increase tax collection, which still relies heavily on income from petroleum, yet insufficient, because among other things, it failed to modify the incentive scheme between the central government and the states referred to above. Not even the "democratic bonus" of the recently elected president was enough to promote a reform of this nature.[26]

The dilemmas and resistance that Fox encountered at the start of his administration will continue to plague him during the second half of his term. The midterm elections produced a Chamber of Deputies with no absolute majorities, while the Senate, which is reelected every six years, will continue to have a PRI majority. The interests opposed to reform are well aware that the president is intimidated by their shows of force, which include threats of strikes, protests, and other violent actions. The question is whether President Fox is prepared for what is to come and whether he has learned from his first three years in power.

The government must decide exactly what it wishes to achieve during what remains of its term: Does it want to continue reforming the economy or retreat? It will also have to declare its position on traditional corporate structures: Will it tolerate, fight, or negotiate with them? Its relationship with the PRI is no less important: Does it wish to govern jointly with the party or fence it in? Although President Fox cannot and should not be expected to have the capacity to impose policy as easily as previous presidents, he should be able to exercise the same type of leadership he demonstrated when he united the majority of Mexicans behind the goal of defeating the PRI.

At this stage, it is difficult to be optimistic about Fox's future performance. The most one can expect are partial reforms, whittled down by a legislative branch that is unlikely to be willing to shoulder the costs of painful or unpopular measures, such as those involving taxes or electricity. In this respect, if reforms are approved in these sectors, their scope will be limited. The aim will be to demonstrate results, but without paying the cost of more profound reforms that would alter the status quo. Labor reforms are a good example of the type of reforms that could be approved. These could, for example, include positive steps, such as increasing the flexibility of hiring terms and the mobility of workers within firms, but stop short of promoting trade union democracy or reducing the costs that the current law imposes on firms—both measures that are imperative for Mexico's political and economic health. The catalyst for agreements of this kind will be the upcoming competition for the presidency, which will force parties to make an effort to look good by achieving results.

Expectations of triumph by the three main parties in the 2006 elections create opportunities that did not exist during the first three years of the administration. There will be an incentive to leave the economy in good shape for when one of them assumes the presidency, but it will be difficult to advance on so many fronts with the speed that the economy requires. Economic reform in Mexico will probably be characterized by incremental steps and partial measures.

The opportunity that Vicente Fox's victory presented for the reform agenda seems to have vanished. Mexicans must accustom themselves to a permanent transition and to an economy that is open to competition yet protects strategic sectors. Unfortunately, Mexico is unlikely to see a repeat of the combination of the desire for reform, which implies a sense of direction and clarity of objectives, and the political means to achieve this that characterized the years of Carlos Salinas's administration. As a result, Mexicans will continue to pay for the costs of a partial reform for many years to come.

Notes

1. I would like to thank the editors for their insightful comments on preliminary versions of the chapter. I am particularly grateful to Dr. Roberto Newell, with whom I had stimulating talks that formed the basis of the chapter, and to Gabriela Campuzano for her valuable contributions throughout.

2. According to Robert Kaufman, the concept of corporatism is most easily understood when it is contrasted with the characteristics of liberal-pluralist societies. In the latter, there are voluntary associations, spontaneously formed and totally autonomous. Conversely, corporatism monopolizes interests, represented by noncompetitive organizations that are officially sanctioned and supervised by state bureaucracies. Ideally, Kaufman explains, corporate systems insert individuals into legally defined associations or organizations integrated into a bureaucratic center from which they draw their legitimacy. See Robert Kaufman, "Corporatism, Clientelism and Partisan Conflict: A Study of Seven Latin American Countries," in James Malloy (ed.), *Authoritarianism and Corporatism in Latin America,* Pittsburgh: University of Pittsburgh Press, 1977, p. 111. In Mexico, corporatism protected, controlled, and incorporated individuals into the political system through what were initially labor and peasant organizations. These corresponded to "associations of compulsory membership that were noncompetitive, hierarchically arranged, restricted to official recognition and differentiated according to the economic activity of organized groups." Corporate entities supported the government in return for having some of their demands met. The official party thus monopolized the representation of organized groups and, through mobilization and political control, managed to strengthen and legitimize the regime.

3. Jesús Silva Herzog, Márquez, *El antiguo regimen y la transición en México*, Mexico City: Planeta/ Joaquín Mortiz, 1999, p. 130.

4. Carlos Salinas de Gortari, *Sexto Informe de Gobierno*, Mexico: Presidencia de la República, 1994.

5. José López Portillo, *Cuarto Informe de Gobierno*, Mexico: Presidencia de la República, 1980; Carlos Salinas de Gortari, *Sexto Informe de Gobierno,* Mexico: Presidencia de la República, 1994.

6. Carlos Salinas de Gortari, *Sexto Informe de Gobierno*, Mexico: Presidencia de la República, 1994; Vicente Fox, *Segundo Informe de Gobierno*, Mexico: Presidencia de la República, 2002.

7. Calculation based on Banco de México data: Información Laboral de Indicadores Económicos y Financieros del Banco de México: www.banxico.org.mx/eInfoFinanciera/FSinfoFinanciera.html.

8. Throughout his administration, Salinas had tried to create new bases of political support through the National Solidarity Program, a federal program for combating poverty that, rather than identifying target groups on the basis of poverty indicators, took resources to communities that fulfilled the key condition of being politically organized. The program attempted to build a basis of community and territorial support rather than working through the traditional corporatist structure. The program was intelligently designed and created backing and votes for the executive branch, but it did not advance sufficiently to constitute an alternative means of political organization to the structure that supported the PRI.

9. According to Jonathan Heath, "Mexico has suffered several crises over the past 30 years. Some of these fit what is known as the first generation model of balance of payment crisis, proposed by economist Paul Krugman, due to the presence of a high public deficit. Others fit Krugman's second generation model of crisis, since they have been characterized by mechanisms of self-fulfilling expectations." Jonathan Heath, *La maldición de las crisis sexenales*, Mexico City: Grupo Editorial Iberoamericana, 2000, p. 19. The Krugman texts referred to are "A Model of Balance of Payment Crisis," *Journal of Money, Credit and Banking* 11, no. 3, 1979, and "Are Currency Crises Self-Fulfilling?" *NBER Macroeconomics Annual 1996*, published by Bernanke and Rotemberg, MIT Press, Cambridge, MA, 1996.

10. Heath, *La maldición de las crisis sexanales*, pp. 48–49.

11. Banks were privatized in the early 1990s following the successful deregulation of the sector, which basically involved removing controls on the allocation of credits and lifting the ceiling on the active interest rates. The institutional environment in which recently privatized banks were allowed to operate was not very encouraging. The incentives to take great risks were due not only to investors' desires to recoup their investments quickly but also to lax regulations concerning portfolio classification, related loans, the definition of notes due, and so on. The universal insurance of deposits combined with a primitive supervisory function proved lethal over time, combining to encourage greater risk taking. The economic crisis of 1994–1995 revealed the enormous vulnerability of the banks, which in the space of a few months created the threat of system-wide insolvency. Subsequent decisions were reactive and, although they met the objective of protecting savings, did so at an extremely high cost.

12. These measures consisted of a strict, orthodox stabilization plan to offset the lack of external liquidity caused by a signficant reduction in capital flows. The plan entailed a major cut in the current account deficit and openly acknowledged that the crisis had reached the point of a recession. Heath, *La maldición de las crisis sexanales*, p. 66.

13. President Zedillo had proposed reforming the pension system, which was in a virtual state of collapse at the time. To replace the existing "sharing system," as it was called, the initiative proposed a private, individualized plan. The reform was approved, albeit in a limited fashion. It did not include workers in

the public sector or the Mexican Social Security Institute (IMSS). Moreover, a public institution responsible for providing health services and social security for formal workers in the private sector, which administered retirement contributions for government employees and employers, was given the responsibility of handling one of the Retirement Fund Administrating Companies (Afores), despite the fact that the original intention of the executive branch had been for these to be handled exclusively by private institutions. For further details, see Guillermo Trejo and Claudio Jones, "Political Dilemmas of Welfare Reform: Poverty and Inequality in Mexico," in Susan Kaufman Purcell and Luis Rubio (eds.), *Mexico Under Zedillo,* Boulder, CO: Lynne Rienner Publishers, 1998.

14. Discipline had been obtained and rewarded by guaranteeing access to power in the form of a seat in a federal or local legislature, a governorship or a municipal presidency, as well as bureaucratic positions at different levels of government. The president's control over the political careers of all candidates was eroded as opposition parties gained positions.

15. For example, a recent ruling by the Supreme Court of Justice declared unconstitutional the legal framework established during Zedillo's administration to allow certain forms of private investment in the electricity sector. It has also ruled against certain decisions by the Mexican government to expropriate property and the establishment of certain types of taxes that violate the letter of the constitution.

16. *Estadísticas oportunas de finanzas públicas y deuda pública.* Secretaría de Hacienda y Crédito Público, 1er trimestre 2003.

17. OECD, *Literacy Skills for the World of Tomorrow: Further Results from PISA 2000,* París: OECD, June 2003.

18. Entrepreneurial success has depended solely on the ability of each entrepreneur, his views, and his access to financing. Anyone who lacks these three elements has experienced growing difficulties. There has been no government policy oriented toward creating the conditions to enable the economy to be fully transformed, so that the sectors lagging behind will be able to adapt, emerge from their lethargy, or, if necessary, close in an orderly fashion. Abandonment of policy in this area has led to an extreme form of Darwinism.

19. The arguments in this section were taken from Guillermo Zepeda Lecuona, *Transformación agraria: Los derechos de propiedad en el campo mexicano bajo el nuevo marco institucional.* Mexico: CIDAC–Miguel Ángel Porrúa, 2000.

20. One acre is equal to .4047 hectares.

21. As a method to provide land to the poor farmers of Mexico, communal groupings were treated in the form of communal farms. The Agrarian Reform Ministry created these communal farms, today known as *ejidos,* through presidential declarations. *Ejidos* consist of a defined governing body, land parcels, and members who create an agrarian community or town. The land is divided into two sections. One is communal in nature and is held directly by all of the members in common; this is where the community services and residences are situated. The other is made up of individual parcels, which are held by each member of the community (in *ejidatario* possession); these are normally used as farms. The federal government retains ownership of the *ejido* land and provides that the communities hold and use it under the Agrarian Rules of Mexico.

22. The distribution of land had been a specific response to the demands made during the revolution. The results of agrarian distribution were extremely

significant; nearly 30,000 *ejidos* were created while over 3 million applicants were granted over half of national territory (103 million hectares). However, a striking feature of agrarian reform is that it took seventy-five years to be implemented. This is one of the reasons behind the failure to achieve its economic goals, far less the aim of justice as regards agrarian distribution. The shift from the distribution of sufficient amounts of land to unreasonably small plots took place within an atmosphere of uncertainty. By 1940, twenty-three years after agrarian reform had officially begun, nearly 30 million hectares had already been distributed, benefiting 1.6 million applicants. If land distribution had been halted at that time, when the size and quality of the land distributed began to decline, it would have prevented many of the acute problems now affecting the countryside, particularly the loss of capital for agricultural activities and the low productivity of small holdings. However, land continued to be distributed for the next fifty years. Zepeda, *Transformación agraria,* pp. 36–41.

23. A look at the agricultural trade balance between Mexico and the United States shows that Mexican chilis, tomatoes, tobacco, and broccoli are among the nation's largest exports.

24. The passage of NAFTA brought about the immediate or gradual elimination of tariffs on a broad range of products. Tariffs were removed from some agricultural products, such as onions, bananas, and coffee, in 1994 (Group A), and from most agricultural products by 2003 (Group C). For sensitive products such as maize, beans, orange juice, powdered milk, and sugar, a special tariff removal category was established (Group C+).

> Group A: Goods on which tariffs were removed on January 1, 1994
> Group B: Goods on which tariffs were removed in five equal, annual stages until they were entirely tariff-free on January 1, 1998
> Group C: Groups on which tariffs were removed in ten equal, annual stages until they were entirely tariff-free on January 1, 2003
> Group C+: Goods on which tariffs will be removed in fifteen equal, annual stages until they are entirely tariff-free on January 1, 2008

25. Declarations by the president of the Board of the Mexican Network of Farmworkers' Organizations to the newspaper *El Financiero,* May 12, 1997; note by Lourdes Edith Rudiño.

26. The "democratic bonus" refers to the enormous wave of popularity on which Vicente Fox was swept to power and the political capital he gained for having defeated the PRI after over seventy-five years in power. Early on, it seemed that this tide of goodwill would be enough to enable the president to advance his economic agenda without any setbacks, but the reality proved to be quite different. Fox's popularity did not help him deal with vested interests or create legislative agreements to support his proposals. In addition to popularity, the president required a strategy, political operators to implement the latter, and a clear sense of direction, none of which he was able to achieve.

3

Fighting Poverty in Mexico: Policy Challenges

Juan Pardinas

In the past two decades, Mexico has undergone a process of profound change. Yet despite impressive political and economic transformations, Mexican society remains divided by dramatic income gaps and pockets of prosperity surrounded by poverty. Over the years, progress has been made in strengthening democracy and building a true market economy, but the challenge of forging human capital among the impoverished majority remains daunting.

Most Mexicans have an income that is not sufficient to meet their basic needs. According to a survey published in 2002 by the Secretary for Social Development (Sedesol), the government agency in charge of antipoverty strategy, 51 percent of the nation's population lives in poverty. Unequal income distribution poses a permanent threat to Mexico's political and economical stability. In the context of a young democracy, the lack of expectations for a better future among one-half of the population opens the door for populism and its champions. The best way to secure the future of democracy and open markets in Mexico is to break the generational poverty cycle.

The government's antipoverty strategy combines targeted subsidies with generalized spending on health and education. In some cases public spending has helped reduce poverty, but significant subsidies that benefit the most privileged sectors of the population limit the funds available and the results achieved. The aim of this chapter is to analyze the political context of this social problem and the policy response of the Fox government to date in the face of pressures generated by insufficient resources.

The Poverty Census: Measuring the Challenge

Throughout Ernesto Zedillo's administration (1994–2000), there was an ongoing debate over the best system for undertaking a census of the

poor. An essential prerequisite for effective, long-term antipoverty policies was the establishment of a precise definition of who is poor and the
gathering of data to quantify the problem's dimensions. This discussion
had implications that went beyond methodology, because the outcome
of each alternative measurement would produce a different set of policies. Each side in the debate had its own estimate of the percentage of
people living in poverty and the ways in which public funds should be
used to tackle the problem. In the government's camp, Santiago Levy,
then undersecretary of finance in charge of drafting the federal budget,
estimated that 18.8 million people out of a population of nearly 100
million lived below the poverty line. His theoretical and political neme-
sis, Julio Boltvinik, an academic from the Colegio de México, constructed an index called the "corrected Levy," which set the figure at
more than twice that, or between 36 million and 52 million poor. Levy
and Boltvinik represented the two positions in the public debate over
the number of people living below the poverty line and the government's policy alternatives.[1]

In 1997, using Levy's work as a blueprint, the incoming Zedillo
government launched Progresa, a multidimensional scheme that combined cash transfers to poor households in rural areas with the conditions that their children attend local schools and the family undergo regular checkups at regional health clinics. The program also provided
nutritional supplements for pregnant and breast-feeding mothers, as
well as for children under the age of five. By 2000, 2.6 million families
were receiving an average transfer of $25 per month, which represented
22 percent of their total income.

According to independent evaluations, Progresa has achieved some
important results. The International Food Policy Research Institute, a
development think tank based in Washington, D.C., found a baseline
increase of enrollment in seventh grade of 7.5 percent for boys and 11
percent for girls in the first fifteen months of the program's operation.[2]
Research by the University of Chicago found a 15 percent increase in
the average physical growth of children who joined the program and a
19 percent decrease in the occurrence of illnesses in adults between
eighteen and fifty years old among participating households within the
first three years of the program.[3]

For a quarter of a century the long-term vision for antipoverty policy in Mexico had a horizon of six years. Every *sexenio,* the incoming
president would present a different approach for confronting the issue.
Policies ranged from the oil- and deficit-sponsored food subsidies of the
José López Portillo administration (1976–1982) to radical cuts in social
spending due to dramatic financial restrictions when Miguel de la Madrid

was in office (1982–1988). During the Salinas administration (1988–1994), social policy became the axis of the president's political strategy. With Pronasol, a demand-based antipoverty program, Carlos Salinas, even more than his predecessors, exploited the political assets of the welfare budget. As in the past, the revolutionary credentials of the PRI were legitimized through fiscal allocations for public spending on the poor. Antipoverty strategy became simply one component of the political machinery exercised through the budgetary process.

Progresa was the first antipoverty scheme that aimed explicitly to shield itself from political influence. Traditionally, peasant organizations close to the PRI would negotiate with the government over the social benefits to be provided to their members. During electoral campaigns and on election days, peasant groups would be encouraged or even coerced into supporting the PRI candidates. Under Progresa, financial transfers go directly to individuals rather than to intermediaries, reducing the influence of organizations that might require electoral support for their favored candidates in exchange for social benefits.

It is difficult to claim with any certainty that Progresa, with a budget of $700 million and beneficiaries in thirty-one states and more than two thousand municipalities, is immune to electoral pressure, although the ongoing oversight of media and the Congress certainly provides some guarantee. In addition, the 2000 presidential elections serve as a prime piece of evidence that Progresa has succeeded in protecting itself from political manipulation. On election day in July 2000, the turnout of the PRI's rural constituencies was lower than expected. Without the full support of its strongholds and with massive opposition in urban centers, the PRI had to concede defeat and the opposition candidate, Vicente Fox, was elected to the presidency.

Progresa's success depends on its long-term application, and the fact that the program was designed as a targeted strategy to combat poverty and not as a political tool of the president has made possible its continuity. In a country where every new administration strives to build its own antipoverty policy without leaving a trace of its predecessors' projects, the future of the Zedillo program was clearly at stake after the 2000 election. During his campaign, Vicente Fox's mantra was one of change, but when he arrived in office, he found that the antipoverty strategies he inherited were a tough act to follow. Faced with the dilemma of continuing the program or wiping the slate clean, the man of change chose to walk the path set by his predecessor. In this sense, the most innovative aspect of social policy under Fox has been his vow of continuity.

The Fox administration has reformed some aspects of the policy, including its name (Progresa is now known as Oportunidades). But the program retains the multidimensional approach developed under Zedillo of targeted subsidies combined with obligatory school attendance and medical clinic visits. And, like Progresa, Oportunidades represents an effort to implement a long-term strategy independent of the political party that controls the government. Instead of using funding levels to obtain political results, the program aims to judge the effectiveness of public spending by the social outcomes produced and to create specific strategies to address different segments of the population, according to age and regional criteria.

One important change under Fox is that Oportunidades provides broader coverage than its predecessor; Progresa attacked extreme poverty only in rural areas, while the new scheme has been extended to cover the urban poor. Another improvement is the disclosure of the government's methodology for measuring poverty. Under the Fox administration, a Technical Committee for Poverty Measurement was established and charged with designing clear criteria for determining the number and location of people to be covered by the initiative and identifying the programs that could best help them. The participation of renowned, independent economists and experts not only improved the survey methods but also legitimized government efforts.

The poverty index, produced by this committee, is based on income per day and groups poor households into three categories:[4]

1. Nutritional Poverty. This is the most extreme poverty level of the three categories, covering people who live in households whose income is not enough to cover their basic nutritional needs. This is the equivalent of an individual daily income of $1.70 in rural areas and $2.10 in urban centers.

2. Poverty of Access. This level includes all the people classified under nutritional poverty, plus those who lack access to basic health and education services. This population group has a daily income of $2 in rural areas and $2.70 in urban areas.

3. Resource Poverty. Encompassing the population living under nutritional and access poverty, this category also covers those individuals whose incomes are not sufficient to provide clothing, shoes, housing, and public transportation. Due to their lack of access to insurance or credit, this income rank is vulnerable since its condition might easily decline if faced with any sort of emergency. This group comprises people who earn less than $3 per day in rural areas or $4.50 in urban centers.

In the summer of 2003, just a few weeks before the midterm election, Sedesol announced that, according to the methodology provided by the committee, between the year 2000 and the end of 2002, Mexico reduced the percentage of people living in poverty (see Table 3.1). The percentage of the population classified under nutritional poverty declined from 24.2 percent in 2000 to 20.3 percent at the end of 2002. In the same period, the population under poverty of access fell from 31.9 percent to 26.5 percent and the resource poverty rate dropped from 53.7 percent to 51.7 percent.[5]

The government explained these improvements as a result of the following factors: (1) a minor improvement in real incomes; (2) economic stability; (3) an expansion of social programs such as Oportunidades; and (4) an increase in the value of money orders sent home by Mexican workers in the United States. In the year 2003, the money sent from immigrants exceeded $10 billion, most of it destined for the lowest-income population of the country.

There is little consensus over how to establish poverty levels, and each methodology has its strengths and weaknesses; still, the Fox government took a positive step by establishing a benchmark for assessing the policy challenge. The estimate that 56 percent of Mexicans live in resource poverty was well above previous government estimates and more than double the 25 percent acknowledged by Zedillo's administration. This has led to some concern that an inflated poverty level estimate early in Fox's term could yield misleadingly impressive results by the end of his administration. No evidence has been produced to sustain such a claim, but it is a fact that the poverty index will be one benchmark by which the PAN government's performance will be judged.

To address concerns that the National Institute of Geographic and Informational Statistics (INEGI) is cooking the figures to the taste of the government, there is growing demand in Congress and the media to grant full autonomy to the institution, whose directors are currently

Table 3.1 Changes in Population Living Under Poverty Thresholds, 2000–2003 (in percentages)

Poverty Level	2000	2002
1 (nutrition)	24.2	20.3
1+2 (health and education)	31.9	26.5
1+2+3 (clothing, housing, transport, and vulnerable due to lack of credit or insurance)	53.7	51.7

Source: Sedesol, based on INEGI, National Survey of Income and Home Spending, 2000: http://www.sedesol.gov.mx/prensa/comunicados/c_098_2003.htm.

appointed by the president. Mexicans have a long and well-documented tradition of skepticism toward public institutions, and INEGI's lack of independence has raised some suspicion over the political neutrality of the data and information it provides, including poverty measurement inputs. INEGI is a professional and highly technical government body, but its eventual autonomy would help to legitimize its performance.

Another criticism of the poverty index concerns the relationship between the daily income threshold of resource poverty established by the technical committee ($4.50/day) and the current level of the legal minimum wage. According to Article 123 of the Mexican Constitution, the minimum wage must be sufficient to cover the basic needs of the main income provider of a household. The minimum wage functions as a benchmark for contractual negotiations in the manufacturing and services industries. If the minimum salary were to fall below the threshold of the government's definition of poverty, it would be likely to trigger demands for an adjustment that would affect wage negotiations throughout the economy.

The poverty assessment is notable because it marks the first time a Mexican government has made an open effort to undertake a poverty census with technical assistance from independent specialists. The survey's official numbers have justified pessimistic assumptions, but at the same time have brought a sense of direction to poverty-reduction strategies.

Considering the dimension of the challenge at hand, the right set of policies is a necessary but insufficient step in improving the difficult social conditions prevailing in Mexico. Although Oportunidades represents a serious attempt to break the generational legacy of poverty, according to the program's own estimates only two out of five poor people are covered by it.[6] The need to expand the coverage of antipoverty programs has run up against the harsh realities of scarce fiscal resources and massive inefficiencies in their allocation. Insufficient public funding will be an obstacle for some years to come. This problem is made all the more pressing by the budget appetites of bureaucrats and the struggles of powerful political groups over the funds available for antipoverty policies, education, and health.

Putting Money in the Wrong Pockets

The need to invest in human capital for the underprivileged must compete for a share of the pool of public resources with a vast list of other priorities. Government bureaucracies tend to equate big budgets with policy solutions to the country's problems. In some cases there is a need for massive public investment, but in others, the use of public resources could constitute an unproductive form of social spending. One example of the latter is the widely publicized Plan Puebla Panama (PPP). During the electoral campaign, Vicente Fox proposed a $20 billion program for massive investment in infrastructure that would stimulate economic development in the impoverished region of southern Mexico and Central America. The public relations appeal of the "three Ps" helped garner positive media attention for a candidate in search of votes. There were just two things missing: a policy strategy to give some substance to the sound byte and a generous budget to make it happen.

Halfway through the Fox administration's term, the original PPP investment program has been downgraded to smaller initiatives that are affordable under regional budget constraints. One indication of the program's weakness was the failure to undertake any cost-analysis research of the social benefits of investing in, for example, highways instead of other development projects. The initiative also faced the obstacle of its paltry funding.

Moreover, even if the PPP is ever implemented, it is likely to have only a limited economic impact in some southern Mexican states, given the small size of Central American markets and the low value of trade with them. The gross domestic product of two important Mexican states (Jalisco and Nuevo Leon) is 25 percent larger than the GDP of the seven Central American countries combined, while the value of trade between Mexico and Central America is less than 1 percent of trade between Mexico and the United States.

Since it was first proposed, the PPP has come to look like a blurry campaign promise rather than a sound policy initiative. The fact that the PPP will never be implemented on the scale originally envisioned during Fox's campaign is good news. During the PRI era, a president's determination to pursue an investment project was enough to put at risk the equilibrium of public finances; a lack of resources or uncertainty regarding a project's potential social benefits were not the main inputs into the decisionmaking process. Under those circumstances, public money was spent on ports that never docked a single ship and bridges and highways over which little traffic ever passed.

The recognition that fiscal resources might be better spent on initiatives other than a widely publicized presidential proposal is a big change from the Mexico of the 1970s and 1980s. This is not to say, however, that the allocation of public money is no longer subject to political influence under the Fox administration, especially since special-interest groups that survived the PRI era continue to exercise influence over budget priorities.

Subsidies for Those Who Don't Need Them

Vicente Fox's government inherited a costly list of subsidies that are justified politically as expenditures to help low-income families. The truth is exactly the opposite.

The case of electricity subsidies is a good example of a regressive investment, where the allocation of public funds serves to reduce the energy bills of that segment of the population with higher incomes. In Mexico, two publicly owned companies (Comisión Federal de Electricidad and Luz y Fuerza del Centro) supply power generation for the entire country. Due to the lack of investment in modern technology and low labor productivity, Mexico has one of the most expensive electricity services among OECD members. Through taxes, transformed into subsidies, plus the face value of the electricity bill, a household in Mexico City may pay up to 2.5 times more than one with equivalent consumption in Texas.[7]

One of every three pesos collected through the value-added tax (VAT), Mexico's equivalent of a sales tax, is spent on subsidies to electricity consumers. The combined subsidies for both power companies in 2002 amounted to five times the total budget of all antipoverty programs, with Oportunidades receiving only one-seventh the amount of the electricity subsidy. Two years earlier, electricity subsidies absorbed 15 percent of budgetary spending, while the social program Progresa represented just 2.1 percent.

In addition to the issue of how public resources are spent, there is the question of who benefits from them. According to recent research,[8] for every peso spent on electricity subsidies, the richest 20 percent of the population receives 26.5 cents and the poorest fifth only 14 cents. In contrast, for every peso spent by Progresa, the poorest third of the population receives 90 cents. (See Table 3.2.)

This means that income gaps are wider and distribution of wealth is more unequal every time the government spends a single peso to disguise

Table 3.2 Comparative Distribution of Electricity Subsidies and Progresa by Income Deciles, 1998

	I	II	III	IV	V	VI	VII	VIII	IX	X
Progresa	44.9%	25.4%	23.8%	3.8%	1.6%	0.5%	0	0	0	0
Electricity Subsidies	5.1%	8.9%	8.6%	9.0%	9.7%	10.0%	10.8%	11.6%	11.4%	15.1%

Source: John Scott, www.desarrollotributario.org/presentaciones/scott.ppt.

the real costs of electricity. Poverty alleviation is not just an issue of policy design, but also requires taking the right decisions to allocate public resources in areas that produce the highest returns for society. But any decision to free resources from electricity subsidies and invest them in human capital for the poor is blocked by the political risks involved.

There are a number of explanations for the high price of electricity in Mexico. One is the growing maintenance and operational costs of outdated infrastructure. Four-fifths of generation plants are more than two decades old.[9] Government calculations estimate that the modernization of the power sector in Mexico will need an investment of $50 billion over the next ten years—an amount that could fund Oportunidades up to the year 2071.[10] Under current law, these resources must come from government spending, not private investors. The lack of investment in technology to modernize power generation plants could be solved if laws that forbid private investment in the sector were changed.

Another problem is low labor productivity in the power sector. The large number of employees, their high incomes relative to other blue-collar workers, and the concessions granted to their unions make it impossible for these companies to produce electricity in an efficient and cost-competitive way. For example, in 2002, labor costs in Luz y Fuerza del Centro were five times higher than its gross income.[11]

Since the Zedillo administration, initiatives have been proposed to change the status quo of power generation in Mexico. But due to the current lack of enthusiasm for the market reforms of the late 1980s and 1990s, the opening of the public utilities sector to private suppliers would involve political risks for any government that might try to push such a plan. Opposition parties in Congress have blocked any such change in investment regulations, appealing to currents of nationalism and sovereignty. In addition, the powerful economic interests of electricity unions are well served by figures of speech that use "private capital" and "national threat" as synonyms.

The Fox government is convinced of the virtues of the electricity reform, but has failed to make clear its urgency or to convince the public of the need to choose among competing investment priorities. There is a convincing argument to be made for dedicating public resources to programs that are unlikely to attract private investment. If private investors are willing to build power generation plants, there is little justification for spending scarce public resources on the sector. Nor has the government specified what it would do with the resources that would be freed by electricity sector reform, an action that could help create public support for such a move.

This failure of communication was also evident in 2001 when the Fox government sent Congress a fiscal reform project that aimed to raise tax revenues above the current 12 percent of GDP. Plans for what would be done with the extra income were not outlined. In a democratic nation, it is almost impossible to raise taxes without a clear explanation of where and how the money will be spent. When the government tried to raise the VAT rate for food and medicine, opposition parties set the tone of the debate, criticizing the government for supporting a tax reform that was "against the poor." The administration again failed to defend its initiative with a focused and clear message as to what the benefits of higher tax revenues would be or how they would be distributed.

Another example of policy confusion can be seen in the initiative proposed by the Ministry of Health to retain a zero VAT rate on a selected basket of medicines in order to protect vulnerable groups. The list of medicines was selected based on two criteria: (1) medication used to cure illnesses that commonly affect people with lower incomes, and (2) drugs for the treatment of long-term illnesses (diabetes, AIDS, etc.) that affect patients for the rest of their lives. Even though this tax policy was sensitive to income disparities within Mexico, the general VAT on medicines with limited exceptions was attacked as hurting the poor. Here, too, the opponents of reform set the debate's agenda, while the government failed to speak out against the presumption that the drug tax exemption had its greatest impact on the highest income sectors. The fiscal revenues lost due to the general zero percent VAT rate on medicines benefit the highest income groups (see Figure 3.1). In the year 2000, the wealthiest 10 percent received 26.8 percent of the tax subsidy on medicines, while the poorest 10 percent benefited by only 3 percent. In the case of Progresa, a targeted subsidy, the tenth of the population with the lowest income received 45 percent of the funds. This is a good example of how targeted subsidies are more efficient tools for fighting poverty.

The strongest argument against a reform of a zero VAT on selected drugs would be that the poor allocate a higher proportion of their income to buy medicines and, therefore, they would be the most affected by adding new taxes. This fact is an argument in favor of a safety net that provides free medicine in public hospitals, but it is not a reason to lose fiscal resources by subsidizing prescriptions for people who can afford them.

Not all generalized subsidies are regressive or exacerbate income gaps. Public investment in health and basic education, to which attention is now turned, are two examples.

Figure 3.1 VAT Subsidies for Medicines vs. Progresa
(by percentage of total)

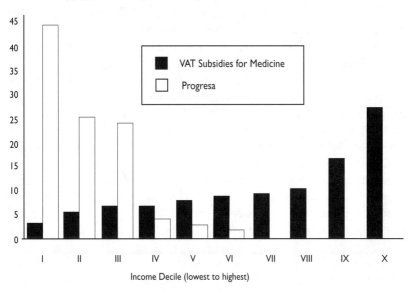

Source: John Scott, www.desarrollotributario.org/presentaciones/scott.ppt.

Education Policy in Times of Change

The social policy of the Mexican government since the Zedillo admin-istration can be described as a combination of broad-based expenditures and targeted income transfers. Public education is a cornerstone of Mexican social policy and the most important generalized subsidy pro-gram in the government budget. For 2002, the allocation for the Secre-tary of Public Education (SEP) represented 16 percent of total public spending. Combined with resources invested by the private sector, Mex-ico spent 6.6 percent of its GDP on education during 2002.

Although education policy has not reached its full potential as a tool for poverty reduction, recent data confirm that there have been some notable achievements. The number of students, including preschool to postgraduate enrollments, jumped from 13 million in 1970 to 32 million in 2002. In the same period, the average number of years of school atten-dance rose from three to seven years. Children who started elementary school in 2002 are expected to complete, on average, 11 grades of school, a significant increase over the 2.6 grades completed in 1960.

The first open confrontation between President Vicente Fox and Mexico's main opposition parties occurred in the initial minutes of his administration. As part of his inauguration address, Fox mentioned in broad terms the issue of education policy—a comment met by shouts of "Juarez! Juarez!" from congressional representatives of the PRI and the PRD. Their interruption was a reference to former president Benito Juarez (1861–1862, 1867–1872) who serves as the national symbol of the separation between church and state. The brawl on the floor of Congress was the result of a cultural clash between a publicly nonreligious PRI establishment and a new government from the PAN, segments of which, since the religious war of the 1930s, have been closely associated with the Catholic Church.

The separation of church and state is a longstanding tradition within Mexico's political system, and secular public education is one of the founding principles of modern Mexico. The Catholic hierarchy has sought to influence such controversial policy issues as family planing and the textbooks used to teach Mexican history. After Vicente Fox's inauguration, members of the PRI and the PRD expressed their concerns about the future of the nation's secular education system under a government headed by an openly Catholic president. In this respect, the first two years of Fox's government served as a learning process for the whole country. After several public statements in which the president embraced nonreligious education policies, the debate was promptly settled. By maintaining unaltered the basic principles of secular public education, Fox proved that a churchgoing president is not a threat to the fundamental character of Mexico's educational system.

The Politics of Educational Performance Indicators

Political change in Mexico has opened a new debate over education policy. During the PRI era, successive administrations measured the success of their approach to education by the growth in access to primary and secondary schools. Key performance indicators included the percentage of young people served by the public school network, the number of dropouts, average years per capita of school attendance, and the number of teachers and schools. Using this kind of data, the SEP's budget became the standard for measuring the educational system's success. Periodically, the government would publish information related to these targets, but data on children's performance at public schools were systematically treated as confidential. The standardized exam results of twelve-year-old schoolchildren were managed like national security documents.

The issue was underscored when the Zedillo government asked the OECD not to reveal the scores of Mexican children participating in the Program for International Student Assessment, published in 2000. This survey of 260,000 fifteen-year-olds in thirty-one countries measured performance in mathematics, science, and reading comprehension.[12] In the overall results of the three tests, Mexican students ranked thirtieth, just above Brazil, which was thirty-first. The OECD survey sparked a debate within Mexico over the need for education policy to focus not just on coverage but also on the quality of instruction.

A key player in the debate over public education is the 1.3-million-member National Union of Educational Workers (SNTE), the largest labor organization in Latin America and one of the most effective pressure groups in Mexico. The union was founded in 1943 as a means of concentrating the political force of the regional teachers' movements that were dispersed around the country. The SNTE negotiates improvements in working conditions and salary increases for its members. Relying on the amount of public spending as a criterion for assessing the accomplishments of the educational system serves the interests of the SNTE, which for years blamed the system's shortcomings on the government's failure to reach the United Nations Educational, Scientific, and Cultural Organization (UNESCO) education spending target of 8 percent of GDP.

In the past two decades, the SNTE has become a political springboard for people seeking positions in the federal government, Congress, and local government. In 1989, Elba Esther Gordillo became the SNTE's chairwoman and promoted a wide range of internal changes in the organization. The most important of these was freedom of political affiliation for union members. Before this decision, unionized teachers automatically joined the ranks of the PRI. The initiative reflected the new pluralism in Mexico and was an effort to provide the SNTE with more political flexibility without loss of its bargaining powers. Dissident groups outside the PRI began to organize and grow, demanding influential positions inside the union's executive committee.

Elba Esther Gordillo ended her term as chair of the SNTE in 1995, but retains strong influence within the organization. Through her informal but visible leadership, she bridges the relationship between the teachers' union and the PRI. Under Fox, Gordillo has been one of the main power brokers in Mexican politics.[13] (Gordillo and Fox met in 1994, when both participated in the Grupo San Angel, an informal caucus of intellectuals and politicians from different parties who sought to influence issues related to that year's presidential campaign.)

Broadening the focus of performance evaluation from budgetary allocations to include the results of standardized tests has the potential to sow the seeds of an educational revolution. The union benefited from the notion that public spending is in itself a performance standard. Lack of educational accomplishments could be blamed on the scarcity of resources, diverting responsibility from the teachers' bureaucracy. The introduction of standardized tests, administered by an independent evaluator, would unmask the need for a change in the union's role from one of bureaucratic control to one that includes support for educational performance.

Other changes are needed as well. The salaries and bonuses of teachers are not linked at all to academic results. Members of the teachers' union enjoy lifetime tenure without themselves being subject to performance evaluations. It is almost impossible to discharge a teacher, no matter what the cause, if union forces intercede in his or her favor. Almost 80 percent of all elementary school teachers receive the same base monthly salary of $700.[14] Salary and bonus premiums depend on location and cronyism within the teachers' union.

Since the end of the 1980s, there has been a significant improvement in teacher salaries. Between 1989 and 1994, salaries increased by close to 100 percent in real terms. In 1995, when Mexico's financial crisis caused GDP to shrink by almost 7 percent, the Ministry of Education was one of the least affected by budget cuts. Since 1996, teacher salaries have risen slightly above the rate of inflation. Elementary school teachers in Mexico City now receive extra bonuses equivalent to 100 days of wages, meaning that they are paid for 450 days per year in exchange for 200 days of actual classroom work.

To become a teacher with a basic wage and access to bonuses, a person needs to complete three years of classroom practice, finish studies in a teacher training school, and pass a test of general knowledge. The union controls teaching schools, as well as the tests measuring the intellectual proficiency of educators. Around three-quarters of all elementary school teachers have decided to join the program to obtain bonuses.

The main problem with the teaching profession is that success depends more on loyalty to the union than on classroom performance. As the education specialist Carlos Ornelas points out, teachers who are more devoted to their classes and students may lose the chance to improve their careers because they will miss union assemblies and events. The teacher's career has become, for many, a professional choice that is closer to politics than pedagogy.

Efforts to link salaries and bonuses to teacher performance have been blocked by the union for years, as it has refused to accept any system of academic accountability. Of course, an organization of the size and complexity of the SNTE cannot be easily labeled. Inside its sixty chapters there are tens of thousands of teachers willing to transform the educational status quo into a system with outside evaluation and bonuses and career advancement based on performance. But under such circumstances, union leaders would lose control over the wage incentive system and, as a result, their wide base of political support would be eroded.

Major Education Initiatives Under Fox

In the first three years of the Fox administration there have been key initiatives to broaden preschool coverage and increase the educational budget, although questions remain over how these projects will be funded.

According to several pedagogic studies, children who enter preschool early are less likely to drop out during elementary education and, consequently, have a higher probability of reaching secondary-level education. One estimate that indicates the importance of education for poverty reduction calculates that for every additional year of secondary education a person's earning capacity increases by 12 percent.[15] Given such assumptions, the spread of preschool education becomes a significant tool of antipoverty policy.

In May 2002, Congress approved an initiative that makes three years of preschool mandatory for children before admittance to primary school. Because the law requires access to preschool for millions more children, the government will need to build new classrooms or recondition schools in order to be able to respond to the inflow into the educational system of children under six. Rigorous enforcement of the law mandating preschool attendance will require a serious increase in spending on education. The legislation established an ambitious calendar for preschool access that imposes prompt government action. During the 2004/2005 school year, five-year-old children will enter the program, followed in 2005/2006 with four-year-olds and in 2008/2009 with three-year-olds. This means that the government has very little time in which to marshal the human and fiscal resources needed for the first stage of implementation.

The SEP reports that, during the 1999/2000 education cycle, preschool coverage was 15.4 percent for three-year-olds, 58.8 percent for four-year-olds, and 82.6 percent for five-year-olds. The population targeted by the preschool initiative totals 6.7 million children, which means that 3.3 million students will be added to enrollment. To maintain the current student-teacher ratio will require 160,000 new preschool teachers. At the current spending rate per student of $850 a year, the government will need to invest an extra $1.5 billion by the year 2008 in order to create the infrastructure needed to enforce the preschool bill.[16] Considering the current fiscal weakness of the Mexican government, this seems an unrealistic goal.

In another important initiative, the Secretary of Education in August 2002 launched a program called the Social Commitment for Quality in Education. This initiative will serve as a benchmark to evaluate the education policy of the Fox administration. The project's philosophy represents a breakthrough in government educational policy because school attendance will cease to be the single measure of success. Furthermore, the policy acknowledges that genuine education reform needs to address the labor relationship between the SEP and the teachers' union. If implemented, one of the more dramatic elements of the initiative is that teachers will rise to become school directors and inspectors through the results of standardized tests and not the backing of the union.

The initiative also promotes the creation of "model schools," where students will have an English-language lab, access to computer equipment, and full-time teaching staff. The initiative will begin with 1,600 elementary schools and is expected to cover the full network of 90,000 public elementary schools by the end of 2006. The Secretary of Education has yet to provide a clear estimate of the resources needed to install computer labs for the 24 million students enrolled in public elementary and secondary schools. Educational reform cannot be reduced to an argument based on quantifying the investment in terms of GDP, but it must be acknowledged that buying half a million computers is primarily a budgetary issue. The lack of a cost assessment for information technology needs in model schools raises doubts about the feasibility of this initiative.

In November 2002, the parties in the lower house of Congress made a desperate effort to improve their approval ratings by passing a law that mandates budget increases for education that will by 2006 reach the 8 percent of GDP suggested by UNESCO. Such an increase implies that 35 percent of all public spending would go to education. There was no debate to explain either the source of funding for this spending hike or the best way to use these new resources.

As part of the Social Commitment for Quality in Education program, the Secretary of Education also proposed the creation of an Institute for Educational Evaluation. For a year and a half the government negotiated with the legislative branch over a bill to establish the institute. Negotiations failed because the Secretary of Education was caught in the middle of a three-way arbitration, trying to satisfy the priorities of government, Congress, and the teachers' union. As a result, the evaluation organization ended up being established by presidential decree without the approval of Congress. In April 2002, during an assembly of the SNTE, the chair of the union, Rafael Ochoa, stated that the organization "is in favor of evaluation . . . but the institution in charge of evaluation should be neither independent nor an autonomous entity."[17] Judging by the content of the presidential decree that created the organization, it seems that the union's wishes were considered in full.

The ultimate design of the evaluation institute is still a matter of dispute due to inconsistencies in government policy. Once created, the new institution was incorporated into the Secretary of Education. This lack of institutional autonomy has raised some concerns about the organization's freedom to pursue its mission. If the SEP bureaucracy absorbs the working process inside the Institute of Educational Evaluation, the new organization may lose flexibility in its administration and management decisions.

But just three weeks after signing the presidential decree, Vicente Fox announced in his State of the Union speech that he would send a bill to Congress granting autonomy to the institute. Considering the government's policy fumbles on several issues, the definitive blueprint for the evaluation body remains uncertain. If the initiative anticipated in the State of the Union speech becomes law, the independence of the institute would be a major setback for the teachers' union, but a positive step toward improving public schools in Mexico.

A technical and nonpolitically biased evaluation process for schools, teachers, and students will make possible a comprehensive diagnosis of the state of public education. It will also help to highlight which schools are doing a better job than others and provide evidence for designing general policies based on these particular experiences.

Evaluation is a critical element of educational reform, but it is not a silver bullet. Despite some positive steps forward, the control of the SNTE over the educational system's rigid labor structures guarantees that there is still room for improvement. Evaluation would not affect poorly performing teachers as long as lifetime tenure is retained. The opening of new teaching positions, recruitment, and transfer of teachers among schools currently depends on decisions taken by the union and the SEP's bureaucracy, with parents and school directors having no say over teacher transfers. Alumni of the teaching schools are entitled by law to first consideration over other candidates vying for teaching jobs in basic education. These rigidities in the teaching labor market will be unaffected by performance evaluation, although the information coming from students' test surveys could trigger new waves of educational reform.

The Health System Under Fox

By the end of the Fox administration in 2006, the Mexican population
will total approximately 107 million people, meaning an additional 8
million will be added to the rolls of those needing healthcare coverage.
For this to occur, the Mexican healthcare system will have to guarantee
its financing capacity and improve the cost-benefit relationship of its
services. Despite some advances in overall indicators of average life
span (from thirty-six years in 1930 to seventy-three years in 2000) and
infant mortality (26 deaths for every 1,000 births in 2000, compared to
180 out of 1,000 in 1930), access to and quality of health services in
Mexico is directly linked to regional and income factors.

- In Chiapas, mortality rates from infectious diseases are over three
  times the national average.
- Infant mortality is twice as high in the five poorest states as in the
  five richest states.
- Adult mortality in Oaxaca is comparable to that of India, while in
  Nuevo Leon it is comparable to several European countries.
- The children of women living in extreme poverty are 2.5 times
  more likely to die before the age of one than the children of
  women who are not poor.[18]

Compared to other OECD members and even other Latin American
countries, Mexico's health expenditures as a share of GDP are low. In
1998, OECD members spent 7.5 percent of GDP on health services,
while Mexico spent only 4.3 percent. Moreover, available resources are
distributed unequally within the country. For example, in 1997, the
northern state of Coahuila spent $60 per capita on healthcare, while
Oaxaca spent only $24. In the same year, Mexico City had 226 hospital
beds per 100,000 people, while Oaxaca had only 44.[19] Even within a
single state, disparities in access to health services are worrisome. In the
most urbanized municipalities of Chiapas there is one physician for
every 557 inhabitants, while in the poorest regions of the state the ratio
is one doctor per 3,246 people.[20]

The need to increase funding for a comprehensive healthcare system is accompanied by the equally pressing imperative to improve the
quality and targeting of expenditures. The government has gradually
started to question the benefits of being the main provider of health
services. In his inauguration speech, Vicente Fox asked his fellow coun-
trymen: "If the Mexican citizens have the power to choose their president, why should they not choose their family doctor?" The phrase

hinted at an initiative to change the role of government from a direct provider to the main sponsor of a healthcare insurance system with private and government providers. If it is well designed, a subsidy to private medical insurance can help produce better cost-benefit results. This transition would require closer coordination among public-sector healthcare providers and a working relationship with equivalent private institutions. The main objective of any such scheme would be to provide improved health services relative to the resources invested.

Although initiatives for healthcare reform can be found in government documents, they have not been implemented because of political resistance to private entities fulfilling government responsibilities. The healthcare system now functions as a mandatory social insurance scheme financed by government funds and contributions from private employees and employers from the formal sector. Medical services for households working in the formal economy are provided by the Mexican Institute for Social Security (IMSS) and the Institute of Social Security for State Workers (ISSSTE). There is a network of government institutions, such as the state-owned oil company PEMEX or the Armed Forces, that have their own healthcare systems, but the Secretary of Health and IMSS cover that half of the population that makes its living in the economy's informal sector. The policy arrangement assumes that each population group will be covered by one of these institutions. In practice, the fragmentation of healthcare system providers leads to a lack of homogeneity in the services' quality and a drain of resources due to the duplication of responsibilities and the misallocation of existing capacity.

According to the 2000 census, 57.8 percent of the population is not covered by either private or public health insurance. In case of an illness, this sector of the population might not seek any medical assistance due to lack of resources. Under the Fox administration, the Secretary of Health has launched a health insurance regime that aims to cover between 2 million and 3 million poor families who use more than one-third of their annual income to buy medicine and obtain health services. Funding comes from the federal budget and a small contribution from its beneficiaries, with the Secretary of Health allocating resources and evaluating the program's results. Despite being federally funded, however, the service is provided by state health systems. The goal of this initiative is to prevent people from falling more deeply into poverty because they lack the money to treat a simple illness. However, if no extra funding is invested in expanding the network of public hospitals and clinics to cover the newly insured population, the current infrastructure of the public health system will become overcrowded and the quality of the healthcare system might be seriously damaged.

Conclusion

After the process of political change that culminated with the election of Vicente Fox, the Mexican people had high expectations for the prospects of an equally deep economic transformation. If democracy was possible, why could not economic growth and development also be attainable?

In the first years of Fox's administration, expectations of a magic cure for Mexico's poverty challenge grew more sober. The social problem remains one of the most crucial issues on the national agenda, despite some innovations in the government's antipoverty policies. During the PRI era, policy decisions were made behind closed doors. The arrival of a new administration triggered a debate over policy issues that were previously not openly discussed by government officials. Topics such as evaluation procedures in basic education and the poverty census were debated with the active participation of society and academia.

The continuity of the previous administration's antipoverty strategy, based on a comprehensive approach that encompasses income transfers, nutrition, education, and health, was the single most important decision of Fox's social policy. But the scarcity and misspending of fiscal resources continue to limit the investment in human capital for the poor.

As we have seen, the political status quo inherited from the recent past continues to influence spending decisions and policy issues. The determination to confront interest groups that benefit from the misallocation of fiscal resources will be a key issue not only for Fox's social policy, but also for the success or failure of economic performance during his administration.

Finally, poverty reduction in Mexico is closely tied to circumstances beyond its borders. With 88 percent of Mexican exports destined for U.S. markets, the fortunes of economic growth in Mexico, as well as the transition from rural to manufacturing and service sectors, will be deeply affected by the performance of the U.S. economy. Mexico's underdeveloped productive structure will be modernized only as long as the process of integration between both economies continues. As the displaced population from the traditional agricultural system looks for job opportunities beyond their unproductive portions of land, illegal immigration to the U.S. labor market will be an obvious choice for many. The economic cycle in the United States, as well as Mexican economic policy, will influence the speed and continuity of economic growth and, as a consequence, the pace of the fight against poverty.

In 2006, when Vicente Fox finishes his term in office, Mexico will still be fractured by gaps of income and opportunity. The right policies to tackle the poverty problem have been set, although they still need appropriate funding. While the value of good policies should not be underestimated, a crucial determinant in their success will be the rate of economic growth. The Mexican transition toward democracy was not swift and neither will be its path to development.

Notes

1. Julio Boltvinik defined his method of measuring poverty as generous or multidimensional because it included access to a wide range of consumer products, such as toothpaste and shampoo. He labeled Levy's method of poverty assessment as miserly or minimalist because it considered only "the indispensable minimums of biological survival." (See Julio Boltvinik, "Opciones metodológicas para medir la pobreza en México," at http://www.bancomext.com/Bancomext/publicasecciones/secciones/2925/bol.pdf, p. 4.) Boltvinik's broader measure highlighted the issue of poverty in the media, although his technical conclusions were not useful as public-policy guidelines. If general consumption products are included in the threshold to measure poverty, it becomes difficult to define the responsibility of the state toward the destitute. Access to health, education, and nutrition are basic requirements for human development and viable aims for social policy. If consumption goods such as a refrigerator and dental floss (both part of Boltvinik's measure) are included in the basket of products that should be guaranteed in order for individuals to lead a dignified existence, the goals of public policy become both less tangible and less affordable. While Levy's poverty measurement yielded a more optimistic account, his methods were more useful for designing a long-term policy for poverty reduction. His assumption was that resources are limited and therefore should be targeted to the neediest Mexicans.

2. International Food Policy Research Institute (IFPRI), *Evaluation of Progresa:* http://www.ifpri.org/themes/Progresa/Progresa_report.htm.

3. Rodrigo García Verdú, *Resumen de los Resultados de la Evaluación del Progresa:* http://home.uchicago.edu/~rgarciav/research/presentations/resultados.pdf.

4. See "Día Internacional Para la Erradicación de la Pobreza": http://www.inmujeres.gob.mx/estadistica/Diadelaerradicaciondelapobreza.pdf. The index is based on the National Survey of Income and Household Spending, produced by the National Institute of Statistics, Geography and Computer Sciences (INEGI), the government bureau in charge of census and official data banks. This biannual survey has been made since 1992. In 2000, it covered a sample of 10,108 households, with 42,000 inhabitants in rural and urban areas.

5. http://www.terra.com/actualidad/articulo/html/act156541.htm.

6. Author's calculation based on data from Sedesol (2002): http://www.sedesol.gob.mx/prensa/comunicados/c_098_2003.htm.

7. Data for the year 2000. For methodology, see César Hernández, *Las sombras de la reforma eléctrica:* http://www.cidac.org/cidac_opina.htm.

8. John Scott, Centro de Investigación y Docencia Económica (CIDE), "Impacto redistrivutivo del gasto público": http://www.desarrollotributario.org/presentaciones/scott.ppt, p.11.

9. See Hernández, *Las sombras de la reforma eléctrica.*

10. This calculation is based on Oportunidades' budget of $700 million for the year 2000.

11. See Hernández, *Las sombras de la reforma eléctrica.*

12. OECD, Organization for Cooperation and Development, *Programme for International Student Assessment* (PISA): www.pisa.oecd.org.

13. In the first days of December 2002, a rebellion of the majority of PRI deputies ousted Elba Esther Gordillo from her leadership in the Lower Chamber. At the time this book went to press (Jan. 2004), it was not clear if she would retain her position as secretary general of the PRI or even if she would be expelled from the party.

14. Carlos Ornelas, "Paradojas del salario magisterial," *Reforma,* May 19, 2002.

15. Susan Parker (1999) quoted in García Verdú, p. 60: http://home.uchicago.edu/~rgarciav/research/presentations/resultados.pdf.

16. Moisés Domínguez, *Retos presupuestales de la educación en el 2003*: http://www.observatorio.org/colaboraciones/dominguez.html.

17. Carlos Ornelas: http://www.santillana.com.mx/Santillana/notiehisto/35.htm.

18. Marcelo Giugale, Oliver Lafourcade, and Vinh H. Nguyen (eds.), *Mexico: A Comprehensive Development Agenda for the New Era,* Washington, DC: World Bank, 2001, p. 412.

19. Ibid., p. 415.

20. Julio Frenk, "Chiapas: Las desigualdades internas," *La Jornada,* January 26, 1988, p. 7.

4

Fox's Foreign Policy Agenda: Global and Regional Priorities

Andrés Rozental

During the first half of President Vicente Fox's administration, critics and supporters alike generally agreed on one fact: the single area of real change since Fox took power in December 2000 has been Mexico's foreign policy agenda. This consensus relates both to the substance of the agenda, as well as to the style of its implementation. For many decades, Mexicans had been led to believe by successive PRI governments that the country's foreign policy enjoyed a broad national consensus; yet, by the time Fox was elected it had become clear that even if this was historically correct, it was no longer the case. Whether on issues of relations with the United States, Mexico's participation in the United Nations, or regional priorities, an increasingly public debate on the country's foreign policy reflected the existence of divergent viewpoints and priorities within different political, economic, and social sectors, as well as among actors directly involved in the debate.

To analyze the international agenda under Fox and assess whether or not its implementation has been a success, one must briefly review the outlines of the new government's foreign policy priorities. These were enunciated in statements made immediately following the July 2000 election by the president-elect and his foreign minister–apparent, Jorge Castañeda, and in the 2000–2006 National Development Plan, all of which affirmed that Mexico's foreign policy should both reflect the clear mandate for change expressed by millions of Mexicans in the polling booth and serve as a tool to anchor the country's transition to democracy.

During his campaign, President Fox had expressed the conviction that Mexico's foreign policy urgently needed to be updated in order to respond more effectively to changing national and international circumstances. The realization that Mexico, the world, and the relationship between the two had changed significantly over the past decade became a central issue during the transition period between Fox's election in July and his inauguration in December 2000. The traditional foreign policy principles enshrined in the constitution—mainly nonintervention in the internal affairs of states, self-determination, and the peaceful settlement of disputes—had been utilized over and over again to justify the country's positions on almost all international issues. For the incoming administration, these gave way to an increased emphasis on Mexico's interests, resulting in a new series of foreign policy challenges for the president. These challenges were in turn translated into six basic objectives to be met by the Fox government during its *sexenio*.

The first objective was to project a different image of Mexico to the world. While the international community perceived that the country had undergone important political and economic transformations, Mexico was largely seen as not having been able to consolidate its democratic agenda and as being faced with ongoing problems of instability, violence, and insecurity. Seventy-one years of uninterrupted rule by the PRI had given Mexico the honor of being the longest-lived "democratic dictatorship" in the world. According to Fox, unless this image was changed it would be impossible to insert Mexico into the international arena. One of the ways of changing this image would be to reformulate how Mexico was perceived abroad by emphasizing its history, culture, and art as a means of enhancing its position on the global stage.

A second objective was the promotion of democracy and human rights as universal values in countries and societies throughout the world. This objective transcended the foreign policy agenda because President Fox was committed to these fundamental values as inherent to every progressive society, and long overdue for Mexico. Strengthening them at the international level would contribute to their consolidation within Mexico.

The third objective was to refocus Mexico's relationship with North America through the establishment of a new dialogue with its two neighbors to the north so as to better reflect Mexico's interests and priorities. Several specific goals were identified, including a necessary and important review of the migration agenda in order to negotiate a landmark agreement with the United States.

A fourth priority of Fox's foreign policy agenda was to promote respect for and defend the interests of Mexicans in the United States. Approximately 20 million Mexican citizens live abroad and, with the largest consular network in the world, Mexico is in a unique position to aid them. However, given the sheer numbers involved, it is impossible for consular officials to assist everyone in need. It has become increasingly difficult for Mexicans without proper documentation in the United States to defend themselves against exploitation and the violation of their basic rights. Therefore, an agreement with the United States to channel the movement of people across the border through orderly and lawful means, as well as to legalize those in an irregular situation, was seen as the only possible way to ensure that these individuals are afforded their rights under U.S. law.

The fifth stated objective was to give Mexico a more active profile within the multilateral system. An immediate step was the announcement of Mexico's candidacy for election as a nonpermanent member of the United Nations Security Council as part of a strategy to invigorate the country's presence in the UN and show that Mexico was ready to pull its weight in the global arena.

A sixth goal was to fully integrate Mexico's foreign policy into the economic development objectives of the 2000–2006 National Development Plan. This was to be accomplished principally through strengthening and promoting Mexico's international economic and trade activity. All Mexican government representatives abroad were relocated within a single building and their activities were brought under the Foreign Ministry's control; the government's multilateral trade-negotiating team was transferred to the Foreign Ministry; and investment and trade promotion were made a fundamental part of diplomatic activity.

A number of additional goals were announced when Foreign Secretary Jorge G. Castañeda took office. Notwithstanding his lack of previous diplomatic experience, the academic, intellectual, and political critic brought many new ideas to the foreign policy agenda. These included reforming and modernizing the country's Foreign Service; reviewing Mexico's international treaty obligations and multilateral commitments to ensure that they were being complied with; bringing greater transparency to the foreign policy decisionmaking process; and maintaining a constructive dialogue and relationship with the legislative and judicial branches of government. Castañeda resigned in January 2003, after just over two years in the Fox cabinet, during which time his extremely close personal relationship to the president brought foreign policy to the forefront of Mexico's new administration.

Many of these objectives were accomplished during those first two years. A new Foreign Service law was passed by Congress, and the Senate approved several major international treaties that Mexico's executive adhered to during 2001 and 2002. For the first time in years, foreign policy became a hotly debated subject in Mexico's media and in public opinion. Ambassadorial appointments became issues of general concern and international affairs assumed an unprecedented degree of importance in the government's early actions. It is against this novel environment that Fox's foreign policy agenda needs to be judged.

Mexico's Image Abroad

Any country's image outside its borders is primarily a reflection of its image at home. For many developing countries however—and this is especially true in Mexico's case—it is difficult to ensure that foreign media and public opinion are attentive to the significant changes being promoted and undertaken internally. Nonetheless, Mexico's common land border with the United States and the presence in that country of millions of Mexican citizens make Mexico's image in the United States of critical importance to the well-being not only of temporary or permanent migrants, but also of the 100 million Mexicans who live in Mexico.

The election of Fox was seen outside the country as the projection of a "new" Mexico. From the beginning of his administration, President Fox and his team decided that it was vital for Mexico to improve its image abroad by capitalizing on his election as proof that the nation had changed. This would serve two purposes: to give Mexicans residing in the United States a sense of pride in their country of origin, and to herald Fox's achievement in removing the PRI from the presidency after seventy-one years of single-party rule. Mexico-watchers were to be encouraged to take a fresh look at the country and its new administration. The improvement in Mexico's image abroad was expected to translate into a heightened interest in further expanding trade and foreign investment beyond the original goals of the North American Free Trade Agreement (NAFTA), thus contributing to another of the foreign policy objectives set by the Fox government: the country's economic and social development.

Another way of improving Mexico's image abroad was through the use of its history and culture as an element of "soft" power to project the country's stature beyond its borders. A new generation of Mexican artists, writers, musicians, film directors, and other cultural representatives were given prominent positions in embassies and consulates. The Mexico Institute was established as an independent government institution, linked to the Foreign Ministry, with objectives similar to those of the British Council, Germany's Goethe Institute, or Spain's Cervantes Institute—exhibiting and promoting Mexican culture, art, education, science and technology, research, and the export of cultural products. Major Mexican artistic and cultural exhibits were assembled and placed in the finest foreign museums and institutions in London, Berlin, Tokyo,

Rome, and several cities in the United States. Special emphasis was given to this objective in locations with large Mexican communities so they could share in the sense of pride and respect for their cultural heritage.

Early in his administration, Vicente Fox also undertook a major effort to change international perceptions of the situation in Chiapas, which had been a festering wound in Mexico's image abroad, especially in Canada and Europe. Allowing and even promoting Zapatista ambitions to bring their cause to the country's capital, the government organized a huge media event that took the movement's leadership on a cross-country trek to Mexico City. There, Congress was urged to initiate a dialogue with the rebels and Fox promised to respect the results of the agreement negotiated with the Zapatistas by the previous Zedillo administration. These measures had the immediate effect of defusing the Chiapas situation in the eyes of foreign observers and showing the world that the Mexican government was not persecuting or fighting the Zapatistas, but rather endeavoring to meet their concerns and reincorporate them into society. Although Congress in the end did not accept the full set of demands that had been agreed to by the Zedillo government, Fox was seen both at home and abroad as having made a serious effort to meet the rebels more than halfway. Although one can question whether the situation in Chiapas is better today than when the Zapatistas rose up in January 1994, Fox's strategy certainly led to a significant improvement in Mexico's image abroad.

In a world where true leadership is a rarity, the arrival of a dynamic, dashing former Coca-Cola executive who had beaten the odds and managed to oust the longest-serving political dynasty of the twentieth century was seen by foreign observers as an event of major proportions. Media attention to Mexico and Fox multiplied and many heads of state and government, as well as dozens of international personalities, visited President Fox in the first two years of his *sexenio* to signal outside interest in the significant political event that had taken place in Mexico. By the third year, however, Fox's attraction began to fade. Unable to make good on many of his campaign promises because of congressional opposition, inflated expectations, and a lack of leadership, Mexico's first opposition president began to look weaker and less promising than at the outset of his administration.

Democracy and Human Rights

The defense of democracy and human rights had been an integral part of the platform of the PAN in its opposition role, and from the start of his campaign as PAN candidate for the presidency these values played a significant role in Fox's own political message. One of the first measures taken by the incoming foreign minister in December 2000 was to create a new, high-level undersecretary for Human Rights and Democracy Affairs within the Foreign Ministry and to appoint a well-known defender of human rights as its head.[1] This was followed shortly thereafter by the appointment of a second undersecretary with direct responsibility for the new global agenda, including environmental, gender, indigenous peoples, and nongovernmental organization (NGO) affairs.

Mexico was invited to join the Convening Group of the Community of Democracies and took the decision to adhere to the Statutes of the International Institute for Democracy and Electoral Assistance (IDEA). Both initiatives are independent democracy-promotion organizations supported by the international community. These two actions, occurring at the outset of the Fox administration, were further indications of the seriousness of its commitment to strengthen democracy within the country as well as internationally.

As part of the new government's pledge to cooperate more closely with international human rights organizations, an ambitious technical cooperation agreement was signed with the UN High Commissioner for Human Rights to undertake a diagnostic evaluation of the human rights situation in Mexico. After years of refusing repeated requests by the International Committee of the Red Cross to establish a regional office in Mexico, such an office was set up with the acquiescence of the Ministry of Defense. Finally, the executive branch proposed the ratification by the Mexican Senate of more than a dozen international treaties related to the protection of human rights and dignities, including a constitutional amendment, later adopted, that allowed Mexico to ratify the statutes of the International Criminal Court (ICC).

Fox also set up a special office within the presidency to maintain relations with NGOs and Mexican civil society. Invitations were extended to several of the UN's and Organization of American States' (OAS) special rapporteurs and commissions charged with overseeing aspects of human rights. Within the context of the inter-American system, Mexico actively promoted and participated in the drafting and approval of the OAS Democracy Charter as an important step in highlighting the new government's interest in defending democracy and human rights in the region.

One of the first expressions of Mexico's new activist foreign policy in the promotion of human rights beyond its borders was the Fox government's position on Cuba at the annual UN Human Rights Commission meeting in Geneva in the spring of 2001. After many years of maintaining a generally defensive posture on this difficult issue—an effort to accommodate both increasing international dissatisfaction with the human rights situation in Cuba and Mexico's traditional opposition to the U.S. embargo against Cuba—Foreign Minister Castañeda addressed the Geneva meeting as follows:

> I am here on behalf of a new Mexico. For the first time in recent his-
> . tory, an opposition candidate was elected President, ushering in a gov-
> ernment for whom the fundamental rights of individuals are a matter .
> of priority . . . [with] the protection of human rights as one of his chief
> concerns. . . .
>   It has been said that the defense and furtherance of human rights
> is a matter pertinent to the internal affairs of each country. . . . Mexico
> does not share this opinion and categorically asserts that human rights
> constitute values that are both absolute and universal. By virtue of
> being absolute, they cannot be conditioned by anyone. They are nei-
> ther internal nor external—they are human. . . . The exercise of sov-
> ereignty cannot be used as an excuse to justify any violation of rights
> which, owing to their fundamental and transcendental nature, take
> precedence over it.

With this policy statement, Mexico abandoned a decades-old policy of insisting that human rights issues belonged solely to the internal competence of states and instead brought them to the fore of its foreign policy agenda. After several unsuccessful attempts to persuade both the United States and Cuba to be flexible in their respective approaches to the debate and to try for a more acceptable resolution of the human rights situation in Cuba, Mexico voted in favor of a fairly innocuous text calling for the Cuban government to cooperate with the commission's special envoy. Mexico's vote infuriated the Castro regime and led it to mount a well-orchestrated attack on Mexico's new foreign minister, who already had a history of disagreements with the Cuban government.[2]

Mexico's change of position at the UN, together with statements by both Castañeda and Fox critical of Cuba's refusal to cooperate with the Human Rights Commission, set off a firestorm within Mexico. Traditional PRI and PRD defenders of the Cuban Revolution and of the Castro regime raised a hue and cry over this supposed change of position, ignoring the fact that it was under two previous PRI administrations that Mexico had begun to shift its Cuba policy by meeting with leaders of the opposition in Havana and Mexico City and forgoing the traditional presidential state visit to the Caribbean island. Fox did, however, go considerably further than his two predecessors in using the Cuban agenda as a clear reflection of the new government's interest in domestic human rights. Fox's dislike of Castro's authoritarian rule and Castañeda's history of antagonism toward the Cuban leader both contributed to making Mexico's Cuba policy an early sign of change from the past.

As to the argument often expressed by Mexican apologists for the internal Cuban situation, Castañeda went on to say:

> We likewise reject the excuse which some States have used to attempt to justify the violation of human rights by pleading *hostility* or *foreign aggression*. With total conviction, we maintain that it is invalid to curtail the human rights of any society or violate its fundamental liberties under the guise of *"State* versus *foreign interests"* since there are neither legal nor ethical grounds to support this. As stipulated in the Geneva Convention, no external hostile action—not even war, nor isolation, nor blockading, nor ostracism—can justify violating the fundamental rights of a human being. Once again, the observance of human rights cannot be conditioned.

The bitter debate that followed in Mexico, mainly within a small but vocal group of intellectuals and left-leaning media, clearly showed that there was no national consensus on this issue. Many Mexicans still believed that whatever went on in Cuba could be justified because of the political and economic isolation imposed by the United States on the island for the past forty years.

The Cuban issue came up again during the UN Summit on Financing for Development that was held in Monterrey in March 2002. Largely in order to preclude Castro from turning the gathering into a showcase for his personal agenda, as well as to avoid a direct confrontation between President George W. Bush and Fidel Castro at the meeting, Vicente Fox naïvely asked the Cuban leader in a telephone conversation two days before the event to agree to leave Monterrey after making his speech and before the final session and dinner. Castro agreed and did depart in time but, unbeknownst to Fox, had secretly recorded the conversation. When the transcript was made public several weeks later, it greatly embarrassed the Mexican president, who was shown to have mismanaged the situation and left himself open to ridicule by Castro. The ensuing scandal almost led to a break in diplomatic relations and served to further damage what little was left of one of Cuba's last friendly relationships in the region.

During the first two and a half years of the Fox presidency, human rights and democracy continued at the forefront of the foreign policy agenda. Largely as a result of Cuba's decision to jail a large group of dissidents and execute three would-be hijackers of a small passenger ferry, Mexico in 2003 again voted in favor of the resolution calling on the Cuban government to receive and cooperate with a UN special rapporteur.

This time, however, there was little debate in Mexico about how the country would vote and Cuban apologists were forced to bite their tongues in the face of international condemnation of Castro's blatant disregard for human rights.

Recasting the North American Relationship

The third pillar of the Fox foreign policy agenda set out to forge a deeper, broader, more ambitious long-term strategic relationship with the United States, building upon what had been constructed in the decade since the North American Free Trade Agreement was signed, but going much further. The new government wanted to transform the relationship in three directions: placing new issues on the agenda, seeking new interlocutors in the United States, and pursuing a new conceptual framework for the long-term vision of a more integrated region.

Beginning with an unprecedented number of direct meetings between both presidents during 2001—including a high-profile state visit to Washington just four days before the tragic events of September 11—a series of bilateral issues that traditionally had negatively affected the relationship began to be addressed in a more constructive manner by the two governments. These included migration, trade, drug trafficking, and security at the border, as well as third-country issues. It is fair to say that until the tragedies of September 11, a new spirit of understanding and cooperation permeated the bilateral relationship to an extent not seen since the conclusion of NAFTA in 1993.

Migration quickly became the bellwether of the new relationship. During visits to both Canada and the United States shortly following his election, Vicente Fox presented to Canadian and U.S. leaders and the public his vision of how the North American community should develop over the coming decades. Included in that vision was a bilateral migration agreement that would recognize the political, economic, and social realities of labor flows from Mexico to the United States. Eventually, in Fox's conception, this would lead to freedom of movement for people to match the free flow of goods and services already existing under NAFTA.

Since Fox enunciated his agenda, there has been much discussion on both sides of the border as to whether this bold initiative was either realistic or wise. Many in Washington thought that such a proposal should first have been presented informally to the administration before being announced publicly. Others felt that since migration is such a controversial part of the domestic political agenda it was unreasonable to expect the U.S. Congress to approve any substantive change in policy.

Nevertheless, the two administrations *did* take the issue seriously and each named cabinet-level representatives to a High-Level Migration Working Group[3] that was charged with negotiating the basic compromise leading to a new relationship, "assuring that migration between the two countries is orderly, safe, legal and humane, and that it guarantees the protection of migratory workers' rights."[4]

What has often been overlooked in the debate that followed, especially after September 11, is that the migration agenda and the proposal to substantively recast the bilateral relationship was the one issue correctly identified by Fox as being of critical importance to a large number of Mexicans. An agreement to regularize the status of the millions of Mexicans already in the United States without proper documents— together with the possibility of channeling future flows through legal and orderly mechanisms—would allow the Fox administration to pursue other aspects of the cooperation agenda with the United States and bind the Mexican government to cooperate in achieving the objective through its active participation and commitment.

The Mexican government's commitment to work toward negotiating and implementing a comprehensive migration agreement as a single undertaking[5] represented a sea change in the policy of previous Mexican administrations. Conventional wisdom in Mexico considered migration to be a U.S. problem. The ability of Mexicans to work in the United States, with or without papers, produced economic and social benefits for Mexico by serving as a safety valve that reduced pressure on the domestic labor market and helped hide the government's inability to provide sufficient employment opportunities at home. An additional advantage was the billions of dollars in annual worker remittances, one of the country's largest earners of foreign exchange. Mexico had not wanted to negotiate before on migration issues with the United States because it knew that at the end of the day this would imply some form of shared responsibility. For its part, the United States was not willing to negotiate migration issues with Mexico because it believed that they properly belonged to the domestic agenda and were unilateral decisions to be taken as a function of internal politics. This "no-policy policy" had been a fundamental pillar of both countries' attitudes toward migration. It began to change only when the two governments decided in 1995 to undertake jointly a binational study on the phenomenon in order to arrive at a common understanding of the nature, size, and tendencies of migratory flows between Mexico and the United States. (The study was formally published in 1997.[6])

The organized labor movement in the United States changed its position on the issue of migration in 2000, in an effort to attract Hispanic voters to the Democratic Party and to rebuild declining union membership. At a meeting of its Executive Council in February of that year, the AFL-CIO unanimously passed a resolution that expressed solidarity with immigrant workers, calling for reforms that would protect workplace rights and freedoms and hold employers accountable when they exploit immigrant workers. The council also unanimously passed a resolution that called for replacing the current system of employer verification of workers' eligibility to work in the United States with a mutually negotiated agreement that would be jointly administered by the U.S. and Mexican governments. Finally, it urged a new amnesty program and full workplace rights and freedoms for all workers—immigrant, native born, documented, and undocumented.

Alan Greenspan has testified that "immigration, if we choose to expand it, could prove an even more potent antidote for slowing growth in the working-age population. As the influx of foreign workers in response to the tight labor markets of the 1990s showed, immigration does respond to labor shortages. An expansion of labor-force participation by immigrants . . . offers some offset to an aging population."[7]

The growing realization that migrants are a key part of the U.S. economy led the incoming Bush administration to accept the proposition from the new Mexican president that it was time to revise national immigration policy. Five major areas were identified by both governments as crucial components of any negotiated migration agreement: security at the border, economic development in source areas of Mexico, a significant increase in the number of U.S. visas granted to Mexicans, an expanded guest worker program, and the regularization of undocumented Mexicans currently in the United States.

The reason for insisting on a package deal was simple: in order for any new migration agreement to be politically acceptable in the United States, it was necessary for both major political groupings to be satisfied with the result. Democrats, the Latino community, and social activists, including those associated with the Catholic Church, were interested mainly in the political advantage of migrants as future Democratic voters and in improving the lives of the millions of undocumented Mexicans already in the country. Republicans, conservatives, and employers were mostly attracted by the temporary worker program.

Unfortunately, the attacks of September 11 put an end to whatever progress had been achieved on the migration agenda, with priorities in the White House, State Department, and Congress rapidly shifting to the war on terrorism and other, more pressing issues. A window of opportunity that had been opened by both administrations to take a new look at the migration agenda was abruptly closed, not to reopen until early

January 2004 when President Bush announced his unilateral immigration reform policy.

Although a bold idea, the U.S. president's new initiative is clearly
less than what Mexico and the Fox administration had originally
expected. Not only was it not the result of a bilateral negotiation, but it
lacks crucial detail and does not directly address some of the main concerns expressed by Mexico and the Hispanic community in the United
States. No clear indication is given, for example, on whether entrants
into a guest worker program such as the one proposed would also have
the opportunity to earn permanent residency if they wished to remain
in the country at the conclusion of their temporary status.

Since Congress will have the ultimate say in whatever immigration
reform is finally approved, it remains to be seen whether the Bush
administration will even be able to obtain part of what it has proposed.
Several draft bills recently introduced by Republican and Democratic
legislators will be considered in the coming months as part of the immigration debate that has fortunately resumed after being suspended after
the events of 9/11.[8]

A second major issue signaling a change in the foreign policy agenda
of the Fox administration in regard to the United States was the thorny
issue of bilateral cooperation in fighting drugs. Since 1987, an irritating
and unproductive process had been in place under which the U.S. government annually certified those countries that had (or had not) "coop-
erated" in helping combat the production, transit, and consumption of
narcotics. Rather than proceeding with the unilateral certification
process that had caused a severe deterioration in Washington's relations
with most of Latin America, Fox and his foreign minister were able to
persuade the Bush administration to push Congress to replace it with a
regional, OAS-based Multilateral Evaluation Mechanism.

A significantly strengthened bilateral commitment to cooperate in
the fight against crime, the exchange of hitherto reserved intelligence
between authorities in both countries, and an expedited extradition
process to bring accused criminals in Mexico to justice in the United
States convinced Washington that it was worthwhile to give this new
initiative a chance. As a result, since 2001 the certification process has
been temporarily replaced with a regional scheme based on a multilateral approach and shared responsibility.

Trade conflicts are always part of the relationship between Mexico
and the United States, and the Fox administration inherited a considerable number of ongoing disputes. One of the most visible was the decision by the United States to delay implementation of the NAFTA provisions calling for a gradual removal of restrictions on Mexican trucks
crossing the border. Strong pressure and lobbying by the Teamsters

Union had led the Clinton government to delay implementing this commitment, and Mexican authorities frequently pointed to the issue as proof of U.S. unwillingness to comply fully with NAFTA. Immediately upon assuming office, George W. Bush signaled his intent to resolve this high-profile dispute by complying with the obligation to remove the barriers to Mexican trucks.[9] Other trade disputes were addressed early in the Bush administration, but most of them remain unresolved.

Bilateral water issues also figured prominently in the U.S.-Mexican bilateral relationship throughout the first half of the Fox administration. Years of drought and misuse of scarce shared water resources came to a head in 2002 and early 2003 when Texas farmers exerted strong pressure on their president (and former governor) to get Mexico to pay its water debt from the Rio Grande basin. Although a temporary solution was negotiated in early 2003. Although a temporary solution was negotiated in early 2003 and abundant rainfall alleviated the pressures exerted by Texas farmers for Mexico to fully pay its water debt, a long-term solution to the problem remains elusive. In spite of there being a will on Mexico's part to resolve the debt, there isn't enough water both to pay what is owed to the United States and to satisfy the demands of politically powerful Mexican agribusiness interests.

Notwithstanding the continued existence of differences between Mexico and the United States on a number of issues, the bilateral relationship is probably at one of its better moments in recent memory. Many day-to-day problems are being dealt with routinely by federal, state, and local authorities. Hundreds of thousands of uneventful border crossings take place each day and the flow of goods and services is now worth over a billion dollars every twenty-four hours. Mexico continues to enjoy a generally favorable image in U.S. public opinion, although disagreements over Iraq have had a significant impact on how each country views the other. The decision by Washington to forgo UN support and use armed force against Iraq with little regard to widespread international opposition led to Mexicans asking more questions and expressing increased concern about the wisdom of a closer relationship with the United States.

As for Canada, President Fox made an earnest attempt to engage the Chrétien government and enlist its support for his vision on the future of North America as a community going beyond free trade, combining further economic integration with free movement of people. Although important agreements were signed during Fox's state visit to Canada in 2002—including an expansion and deepening of the only successful bilateral guest worker program that Mexico has—the Chrétien government showed little interest in looking beyond the free-trade aspects of NAFTA. Preoccupied as always by its special relationship with the

United States, Canada seems to prefer keeping that relationship un-
tainted with extraneous Mexican issues such as migration, economic
development, and drugs. With the arrival of Paul Martin as Canada's
new prime minister, expectations are high that Ottawa will be more
willing to support the larger vision and work with Mexico on its implementation. Although at the Monterrey Summit of the Americas in early
2004 Martin unexpectedly did not join Presidents Bush and Fox in calling for a new North American Initiative; this may have been more due
to domestic politics and upcoming elections in Canada than to fundamental opposition to the concept itself.

The close interdependence among the three economies and societies
of North America presents a challenge for transforming the relationship
into a community of interests that goes beyond the exchange of goods
and services and promotes new areas of harmonization and integration.
Discussions among academics and think tanks have recently begun to
address issues of a common energy strategy, a common currency, and
common market schemes in specific sectors such as steel.[10] However,
the Fox agenda was much more ambitious in concept. In contrast to the
building-block approach of small, sequential steps leading to more de
facto integration, Fox envisioned a North American community that
would reflect from the beginning an intentional, political decision by
the three countries' leaders to work toward this ultimate goal. Therefore,
by this stage, Fox had expected more concrete agreements on moving
forward. The fact that this had not happened is due, in large part, to the
lack of an organized NAFTA constituency in all three countries and to
both the United States and Canada being preoccupied with other, more
pressing issues. Within the region, discussions on a common security
agenda for the hemisphere and a future Free Trade Area of the Americas
have also been overshadowed by other priorities.

The decision by Canada to negotiate a bilateral border agreement
with the United States immediately after September 11, instead of using
NAFTA to enter into a trilateral discussion involving both land borders,
severely undermined the North American agenda.[11] Discussions on a
common energy strategy—one of the three governments' early shared
priorities—have been put on hold after a promising initial study to identify the region's resources and potential synergies.

Mexicans in the United States

Traditionally, many of those citizens who for one reason or another
left Mexico to seek a better life in the north looked down on their country of origin and perceived it, rightly or wrongly, as poor, corrupt, and

unreliable. However, local cultural values are deeply engrained in all Mexicans, no matter where they live or whatever their circumstances for leaving in the first place. It was these strong ties to Mexico that the Fox government decided to strengthen even further by establishing a special bureau in the president's office to liaise with the Mexican community abroad, primarily with Mexican-Americans in the United States.

Although not strictly a part of the bilateral agenda, problems relating to the status of Mexicans in the United States, especially those who enter illegally, play a very important role in defining perceptions on both sides of the border. The fact that a visible number of their fellow citizens are mistreated in the United States, or die while trying to cross the border, is seen by many in Mexico as a reflection of an inherently anti-Mexican sentiment and as a lack of commitment by U.S. authorities to deal with the smuggling rings that prey on undocumented migrants. Although a large number of Mexicans enter the United States legally, the avenues for doing so are very limited and time-consuming. Mexicans consider U.S. policy on both legal and illegal immigration to be essentially self-serving: when the economy requires abundant, cheap labor from Mexico, U.S. authorities are much more lax in enforcing the rules than when unemployment is high or the economy in recession.

The Mexican Foreign Ministry has long been engaged in trying to help Mexicans in the United States through its network of forty-six consulates and agencies in almost half the states. More than two-thirds of Mexico's diplomatic service is engaged in consular protection work in the United States, but the sheer number of people that demand their services overwhelms the limited human and financial resources available for the task. Over the years, several policy initiatives have been undertaken by Mexico to alleviate the plight of the mostly undocumented universe of its citizens abroad. In addition to increasing the number and resources of the consulates, reforms were made to Mexican laws allowing the retention of Mexican citizenship by those who acquire another, and putting in place a scheme to welcome Mexicans returning to their homeland for holidays.

However, none of these measures has had an appreciable impact on the thousands of Mexicans in the United States who must cope on a daily basis with discrimination, underpaid jobs, lack of basic services, and general insecurity because they are in an irregular legal situation. President Fox, a former governor of Guanajuato—a major migrant source state—had experimented with measures at the state level to help those of his constituents who left for the United States. It was therefore not surprising that upon assuming office Fox made the relationship of his government with Mexicans abroad a priority by creating a cabinet-level office in the presidency to deal with their problems.[12]

The single most important development affecting the lives of millions of Mexicans in the United States was the decision by the Foreign Ministry to expand and intensify the issuance of *matrículas consulares:* special identification cards that are given to Mexicans residing abroad as proof of their citizenship. Although they have no formal legal standing in the United States, these IDs have rapidly become indispensable to many Mexicans who, largely because of their undocumented status, have no legal proof of identity or of their Mexican citizenship. State and local authorities, as well as banks, employers, and police departments around the United States, have begun to recognize and accept the *matrícula* as a quasi-official document, allowing holders to open bank accounts, identify themselves to local authorities, and otherwise give proof of their citizenship. By the end of the first half of 2003, 1.2 million of these secure cards had been issued by Mexican consulates and were officially recognized by 36 counties, 119 municipalities, 900 police departments, and 150 banks. From the perspective of the Mexican Foreign Ministry, issuing the *matrícula* has become by far the most important activity of its consular network.

Finally, one of the successes of the Fox administration's commitment to assist the Mexican community in the United States has been the considerable easing of the onerous conditions attached to the billions of dollars of remittances that workers send back to their families in Mexico. Through a combination of pressure on the private banking sector and the opening up of competition among providers of these services, the costs of commissions and exchange-rate losses have been reduced over the past three years by more than half. Although part of this can be attributed to market forces, Fox's insistence on pushing financial intermediaries to reduce their often usurious rates undoubtedly contributed as well.

In spite of all these efforts to improve the relationship between Mexicans in Mexico and the approximately 20 million Mexicans and U.S. citizens of Mexican descent that live in the United States, there is still an undercurrent of skepticism and mistrust between the two groups. President Fox made a valiant attempt early in his administration to include temporary and permanent expatriates in his count of the number of Mexicans over whom he governs, but reality has shown that this aspect of the foreign policy agenda is still largely unrealized.

The Multilateral Agenda

In keeping with its relative size and power, Mexico has always been a strong supporter of multilateralism and international institutions. However, foreign policy priorities had shifted over the years among the bilateral, regional, and global agendas. At one time an important player on disarmament, third world issues, promoting peaceful settlement of civil conflicts, and the strengthening of regional institutions, Mexico's role on the world stage had been reduced significantly over the past decade as it concentrated almost exclusively on its relations with the United States. Abandoning its activist foreign policy, Mexico had chosen to focus on international trade and economic negotiations as a way of inserting the country into an increasingly globalized world, leaving the high-profile political dimension to other players.

From this position of relative isolation, Mexico under Fox decided to reclaim a front row seat in the international arena and to fully participate in, rather than simply observe, the development of the global political agenda. (Previous administrations dominated by the PRI had pursued a largely reactive foreign policy agenda.) This explains one of the first important foreign policy announcements by the Fox government: to present Mexico's candidacy as a nonpermanent member of the UN Security Council for the 2002–2003 term.

The decision signaled Mexico's commitment to return to being an active player on the international scene. It also changed a long-held position of self-restraint under which Mexico had avoided the Security Council[13] largely because of a misguided theory that the Council was where great powers discussed issues of such importance to their vital interests that Mexico was better off not getting involved because it might lead to confrontation with the United States. Proponents of this policy, many of them career Mexican diplomats, refuse to consider the fact that superpower interests are of critical importance to the rest of the world and that ongoing nonparticipation in the Council is akin to abdicating a role in shaping the negotiations and decisions over issues that, sooner or later, will also affect Mexico. Therefore the choice was not between helping shape the agenda or being a passive observer.

Of course, in December 2000 no one could have foreseen that the Security Council would acquire the high profile it did in the debate and decisions surrounding the crisis in Iraq. Even on this extremely controversial issue,[14] Mexico played a significant role in brokering compromise texts in the negotiations that led up to Resolution 1441 and the ultimatum for Iraq to cooperate with UN inspectors. When the Fox administration decided to take a position of principle and oppose the automatic authorization of the use of force, Washington reacted with fury. High-level Bush officials wasted little time in venting their anger at the fact that Mexico did not align itself with the United States on the issue and had even allegedly helped convince fellow Security Council member Chile to oppose it.

Mexico's refusal to back the United States and its "coalition of the willing" had a measurably negative effect on the already shaky bilateral political relationship after the events of September 11. A Bush doctrine that maintains Manichean extremes of being either "with us or against us" doesn't sit well with a country like Mexico that prides itself on an independent foreign policy and has had important historical disagreements with the United States on issues such as Cuba, interventions in Panama and Grenada, and the Middle East. It remains to be seen whether the disappointment expressed by the Bush administration at Mexico's unwillingness to support the coalition against Iraq will have any long-lasting consequences. There can be little doubt, however, that it led to a cooling of the bilateral relationship in the weeks immediately following the conflict.

Jorge Castañeda's hopes, expressed in an article in the *Los Angeles Times* just before the first meeting between Presidents Bush and Fox in Guanajuato in February 2001, were dashed after September 11 and the dispute over Iraq:

> A mature relationship means that both countries can explicitly refer to their common perceptions and agreements as well as to their differences or disagreements. And they can talk about differences on bilateral as well as on regional issues such as Cuba or the Kyoto Protocol on combating global warming. Maturity also means that the long-term objectives of the bilateral agenda will not be jeopardized even if disagreements occur, as they will in a complex relationship. Maturity requires that transparency becomes the name of the game: There must be no embarrassing agreements to hide or carefully glossed-over disagreements.[15]

There were other multilateral priorities during the first three years of the Fox *sexenio:* organizing the United Nations Summit on Financing for Development in Monterrey in spring 2002; hosting the Asia Pacific Economic Cooperation (APEC) meeting of heads of state in Baja California in the fall of that year; holding the crucial Doha Round World Trade Organization ministerial meeting in Cancún in fall 2003; and inviting the region's leaders to conferences on hemispheric security and a summit on the Free Trade Area of the Americas initiative in late 2003 and early 2004. Mexico's leadership in these important events is but one indication of the high priority given by Fox and his government to the international agenda and the country's new prominent role in it.

But the cornerstone of the revitalized multilateral presence pursued by Fox and Castañeda remained the highly visible role of Mexico in the Security Council. In this regard, special mention needs to be made of the sui generis contribution of Mexico's UN ambassador, Adolfo Aguilar Zinser. A close friend of Castañeda, Aguilar Zinser was tapped by the future foreign minister to be part of the international affairs transition team between Fox's election and his inauguration. Together, he and Castañeda became the spokespersons for the incoming administration's global agenda and drew up the plans for its foreign policy priorities. Inseparable at first, the two began to show signs of rivalry in the early months of the new government when Aguilar Zinser was named to the newly created post of national security adviser.[16] After several months of bitter public disputes between the new adviser and the established institutions of government that deal with national security issues, the president decided to eliminate the controversial office and named Aguilar to the United Nations.

As soon as he arrived in New York, the new ambassador informed the media that he would take his instructions directly from the president. Combined with his publicity-seeking nature, this open rebellion against Castañeda profoundly affected the new administration's multilateral agenda. Rather than having the Security Council seat become an administration showpiece, Castañeda sidelined himself from the United Nations during 2002, for all practical purposes allowing Aguilar free rein. This contributed to serious misunderstandings and conflicts between the Mexican and U.S. governments in the weeks leading up to the crucial decisionmaking process on Iraq.[17] By this time, it seemed clear to the inner circles of the Bush administration that Fox and his team were not going to be of any assistance to the United States on the Iraq issue. While Fox and his senior advisers tried to keep both Washington and Mexican public opinion happy—an impossible mission—Aguilar Zinser at one time threatened to resign if instructed to support the armed intervention against Iraq.

In the end, the saga of Mexico's controversial ambassador to the UN ended badly, both for the Fox administration and for Mr. Aguilar Zinser himself. After making off-the-cuff remarks at a Mexican university to the effect that "the United States has always considered Mexico as its backyard," Aguilar was summarily dismissed by President Fox for "having offended the Mexican people and their President." Not one to let anyone get the upper hand, the ambassador spurned an offer to remain at his post for another two months and tended his immediate resignation, not without first firing a parting diatribe against President Fox in the guise of a scathing and irreverent open letter.

Mexico and Latin America

Even before his election as president, Vicente Fox played the Latin American card as an example of his desire to give greater balance to

Mexico's foreign policy. After years of a U.S.-dominated agenda, Fox and Castañeda felt it was time to reemphasize Mexico's place in the region with which it has the greatest cultural, linguistic, and historical identity. Not only did Fox travel to several of the Southern Cone countries during his months as president-elect, but he also began to play an increasingly important leadership role in the region by trying to contribute to solving several of its problems.

In an early demonstration of his desire to differentiate himself from his predecessor, Fox met with then-president Andrés Pastrana of Colombia and offered to resume Mexico's role as facilitator in the decades-old civil conflict between the government and groups of armed guerrillas. As a result of this meeting and of Pastrana's decision to call for greater involvement by the international community in the stalemated talks between his government and the Fuerzas Armadas Revolucionarias de Colombia (FARC) rebels, Fox dispatched the author of this chapter as a special presidential envoy to meet with the FARC leadership and try to develop a blueprint for moving the peace process forward.[18]

After meeting with FARC commander Marulanda and his colleagues in rebel-held territory within the special zone ceded by Pastrana to the guerrillas, I was able to act as an intermediary between the Colombian authorities and the FARC. In addition to conveying confidential messages from one side to the other, my role led me to an equally important mission related to the U.S.-Mexican agenda: establishing a channel for discussions on so-called third-country issues.

Traditionally, bilateral matters have been the most important part of the U.S.-Mexican relationship. U.S. and Mexican presidents and secretaries of state talk about the border, drug enforcement, trade, investment, tourism, and the many other issues that directly affect the two nations on a daily basis. During the Central American crisis of the late 1970s and mid-1980s, the two countries talked sporadically about Central America, but in most cases the discussions pointed to differences rather than to a common vision. However, Fox and Bush decided at their initial meeting in February 2001 that there would be a systematic exchange of information, points of view, and consultation on issues related to third countries that were relevant to both their agendas. As a result, information and intelligence was often shared on issues such as Cuba (Fox tried in vain to convince Bush of the need for a major shift in U.S. policy toward Castro), the situations in Venezuela and Colombia, and the economic crises in Argentina and Brazil. This relatively new role for Mexico was important both for Fox and for the relationship with the United States. It allowed Mexico to be an interlocutor with the United States on matters where it has more information, more sensitivity, and perhaps a better reading of what is occurring than analysts in Washington.

Although Fox showed an early interest in expanding and deepening Mexico's ties with Latin America, at the halfway point in his administration it appears that most of his projects in this respect have gone awry. The conflictual nature of his administration's relationship with Castro has marginalized Mexico's ability to act as an effective interlocutor between Washington and Havana.[19] The Colombian peace process was interrupted by Pastrana's dismantling of the special area and the election of President Alvaro Uribe, who prefers United Nations mediation to either individual or collective multinational facilitation. Repeated overtures to both past and present Brazilian administrations to cooperate more closely on the bilateral and regional agenda have resulted at best in a lukewarm response, while Mexico was unable to contribute anything more than moral support to help Argentina out of its economic meltdown in late 2001.

Even in the OAS, Mexico's early engagement with the important issues of regional integration and hemispheric security appears to have waned as a result of unenthusiastic reactions by other Latin American governments. Argentina's convening of a Meeting of Consultation under the Rio Treaty in response to the events of September 11 was a clear slap in Mexico's face, given the latter's notorious opposition to the region's outdated security pact.

In his desire to find new avenues for the Mexican relationship with Latin America, Fox also came up with the Puebla-Panamá initiative. This was a strategic move designed to link the poorer parts of southern Mexico with the countries of Central America in order to jump-start the economic development of the region through the financing of major infrastructure projects, such as railroads, highways, seaports, and airports. The goal was to attract private-sector and multilateral financial support as an indispensable first step toward providing the infrastructure necessary for domestic and foreign investment in a traditionally shunned region. Although a positive idea, it has thus far been impossible to implement because of the global economic downturn, a lack of interest by the principal international lending agencies, and a lingering suspicion on the part of Central Americans that the strategy is designed less to help them than to inject investment into southern Mexico.

Conclusions

In this effort to summarize the many components of the foreign policy agenda under President Fox during the first half of his administration, it has been necessary to omit several important ongoing initiatives that, if achieved, will definitely mark his *sexenio* as one of change. These include, among other things, Mexico's ratification of the International Criminal Court statutes; participation in the Community of Democracies initiative; an intensive international environmental agenda; deepening ties with Europe and Asia; promoting democracy in Latin America; dealing with new security concerns in the Western Hemisphere; and acting as a partner in the fight against international terrorism.

An overriding question remains: Was Fox's foreign policy, up until Castañeda's resignation in early 2003, driven primarily by Castañeda himself, or was it a Fox agenda? In retrospect, it seems that Castañeda was essentially responsible for most of the initiatives and policies that characterized the first years of the Fox administration. Although his abrasive, confrontational style often irritated supporters and opponents alike, Castañeda undoubtedly gave Mexico's foreign policy agenda a much-needed active profile and clear set of objectives. It also propelled the Foreign Ministry to the forefront of government decisionmaking, due to Castañeda's extremely close relationship with Fox.

Moving from the Economy Ministry to Foreign Affairs, Luis Ernesto Derbez has brought an essentially economic agenda to Tlatelolco.[20] After having opposed the transfer of international trade negotiating authority to the Foreign Ministry when he was in his former department, one of Derbez's first initiatives was to do exactly what Fox and Castañeda had decided on several years earlier, but had been unable to pursue, due in large part to Derbez's strong opposition.[21]

Another change that marked the midpoint of the Fox administration was the increasing sense of frustration regarding Mexico's relationship with the United States. Far from becoming a new partnership promised in the early days of both presidents, dealings between Washington and Mexico City could best be described in the post-September 11 and Iraq scenarios as "back to the past." Not until January 2004, when Bush and Fox met at the Summit of the Americas in Monterrey, was the personal chemistry re-established after more than a year of mutual accusations and recrimination. Although it is still early to pass judgment on whether Bush's immigration reform proposals will successfully pass Congress and give Vicente Fox a much-needed domestic political triumph, the atmospherics of the relationship have once again become positive. Although this doesn't mean that difficult bilateral issues and disagreements over the past year and a half won't continue to characterize the relationship, an improved personal rapport between the two presidents has always had a beneficial effect, and it is possible that the second half of the Fox presidency will see resumed progress on some of those issues.

The Mexican president's own political weakness in gathering sufficient support for his domestic reform agenda will surely continue after his party's poor showing in the midterm congressional elections on July 6, 2003. It is doubtful whether he will have enough strength to make good on some of the commitments undertaken with the United States. Chief among these is the quid pro quo offered as part of the migration proposal to do everything possible, after an overall agreement is reached, to ensure that Mexicans cross the border through authorized channels and with proper documentation as long as there are additional avenues to allow them to enter legally and expeditiously. As was unfortunately evident after September 11 and the Iraq invasion, the underlying anti-U.S. tendencies of Mexico's intellectual left have found the same fertile ground south of the border as the one anti-Mexican forces have been able to exploit to the north. This is unlikely to change in the short term and will of necessity be an important factor in determining the climate in which the bilateral relationship evolves over the next three years.

For his part, George W. Bush still does not appear to need or want an improved relationship with Mexico other than for domestic electoral reasons, most of which have become apparent with his immigration reform proposal directed at the Hispanic vote in November 2004. In spite of the rhetoric by Bush and senior administration officials in Monterrey at the Summit of the Americas, Mexico and Latin America still appear to remain at the low end of Washington's current priority agenda. Iraq, Iran, North Korea, and the Middle East are today much more important in the eyes of U.S. policymakers than the immediate neighborhood. As Richard Haass, former head of policy planning in the State Department and now president of the Council on Foreign Relations, said in a private discussion in Mexico City in April 2002, "Latin America is not a Bush priority because the region is not in crisis, nor is it perceived in Washington as an immediate threat to the security interests of the United States."

During the first years of the Fox administration, public-opinion polls consistently showed strong support for the government's conduct of its foreign affairs. Most of this positive feeling came from the conviction held by many Mexicans that there would be a new, improved relationship with the United States. Although many areas of that relationship are in far better shape today than before, public perception in Mexico is that Mexico and the United States are still distant neighbors with severe limits to their friendship.[22]

Some general conclusions can be drawn from the first three years of the Bush-Fox relationship. As has always been the case, there continues to be a strong asymmetry to the importance given to each of the two countries in the other's capital. Mexico constantly worries about the attitudes and reactions of its neighbor to the north, while U.S. officials often overlook Mexico and its growing importance to the United States. Vicente Fox sincerely believed, based on Bush's campaign promises and early rhetoric about Mexico being the most important relationship for the United States, that he could create a new partnership with the former Texas governor who became president. At the same time, very few officials in Washington—including members of Congress—were really interested or engaged in such a project.

On the Mexican side, a change in foreign ministers contributed to a downplaying of the migration issue as the number-one priority on the foreign policy agenda. Secretary Derbez, in a series of interviews shortly after taking office in January 2003, signaled his intent to push the trade and economic agenda first, with a bilateral migration agreement remaining a priority, but one that could take twenty or thirty years to achieve. Shortly thereafter, the Interior Ministry took over the day-to-day aspects of the migration issue and although there has been a renewed sense of optimism on both sides that progress will be made after Congress considers an immigration reform strategy, it is doubtful that anything specific can be put in place before the November 2004 elections.

• While Mexico initiated a push to re-identify with Latin America, on the economic front events contrived to frustrate that goal with crises in the Southern Cone and a global economic slowdown.

• While Mexico deployed a costly and considerable effort to win its seat on the Security Council, many Mexicans still believe that this was a mistake and contributed unnecessarily to creating more tension with the United States.

• While the multilateral agenda was meant to balance the overwhelming importance of the bilateral relationship with the United States, there still does not appear to be any concrete achievement that would contribute to that objective.

• While NAFTA has continued to increase trilateral trade and investment flows, it has not been possible to focus Washington's or Ottawa's attention on the merits of deepening the relationship and working toward a North American community.

• While September 11 dramatically altered attitudes in the United States toward foreigners, Mexico was unable to capitalize on the marked improvement in bilateral cooperation on behalf of its priorities on the bilateral agenda.

• Until there is concrete progress on the migration front, neither Presidents Bush nor Fox will have truly contributed to re-casting the bilateral relationship and establishing the partnership they both committed to at the outset of their administrations.

• While many of the initiatives taken during the first years of the Fox administration were intended as harbingers of change in Mexico, most of the reform agenda has languished in a stalemate between the executive and legislative branches.

• While Mexico coveted its new position as a strategic dialogue partner with the United States on global and third-country issues, this role now appears to have been taken over by Brazil and its new president.

From the above, one can conclude that the ambitious foreign policy agenda set out by Fox and his Foreign Ministry at the end of 2000 has so far had mixed results. A good number of issues are being dealt with every day in a manner that befits friends and neighbors with common interests. The main agenda for Mexico, however, remains unfinished. Until there is concrete progress on the migration front, with solid gains for opening legal and orderly avenues that benefit Mexicans going to the United States, the Fox administration will be seen at home as having failed in its objective of recasting the bilateral relationship. Until President Bush recognizes and acts upon the importance of Mexico and Latin America to the United States, the region will continue to feel neglected. Until the elements of a true partnership between the two nations are consolidated without recourse to recrimination and coercion, Mexico and the United States will remain friends and neighbors, but not partners.

Of necessity, the period covered by this volume deals only with the first three years of the Fox presidency and therefore represents only half the story. Though there are grounds for both optimism and pessimism in expecting further progress toward moving the foreign policy agenda from where it is today, President Fox has repeatedly insisted that priorities remain as they were enunciated during his campaign and during the first three years of his administration. George W. Bush has in effect said the same. It remains for future analysts to prove them right or wrong.

Notes

1. Mariclaire Acosta, formerly the president of Amnesty International in Mexico, was first nominated by President Fox as Special Ambassador for Human Rights. When the Senate balked at approving the appointment, a decision was made to withdraw her nomination and instead name her as Undersecretary for Human Rights and Democracy, an appointment that did not require Senate confirmation.

2. In 1997, Castañeda published *Compañero: The Life and Death of Che Guevara,* a critical history of the Argentinian guerrilla hero and Fidel's role in his eventual murder in Bolivia. The book was banned in Cuba and led to Castañeda being excoriated by the Castro government and for all practical purposes declared persona non grata.

3. President Fox named Interior Minister Santiago Creel and Foreign Minister Castañeda, while Bush designated Secretary of State Colin Powell and Attorney General John Ashcroft. The group met several times in 2001 and 2002, but has been dormant since then.

4. Joint Communiqué issued by the two governments on April 4, 2001. The document went on to say:

> Both governments envisage this process as an exercise in shared responsibility with a long-term timeframe that will assure that the migration of Mexicans to the United States provides mutual opportunities and benefits. Both governments also reiterated their commitment to an orderly flow of individuals all along their common border, and to their security. They recognized that the various points of the agreed agenda are interconnected and comprise a comprehensive whole with which to reach a meaningful solution to the migratory issue. [U.S. Department of State, 2001 Press Releases, Washington, D.C.]

5. In order to explain this concept—a well-known trade-negotiating term—in more popular language, Castañeda referred to it as the "whole enchilada."

6. Research teams in each country studied each of five aspects of migration within their country and collaboratively analyzed the findings. The main objective of the Binational Study was to contribute to a better understanding and appreciation of the nature, dimensions, and consequences of migration from Mexico to the United States. It also provided an opportunity to identify options to respond to these movements.

7. Testimony of Alan Greenspan, Chairman of the Board of Governors of the U.S. Federal Reserve System, before the Special Committee on Aging, U.S. Senate, Washington, D.C., February 27, 2003.

8. It is interesting to note that progress was quite significant at the technical level. A draft guest-worker agreement was developed by the U.S. State Department's Bureau of Consular Affairs, and the outline of an "earned" legalization program was developed. These documents were hastily withdrawn after September 11, but remain as testimony to the political will to move forward exhibited at the time.

9. Although President Bush signed the respective bill into law in 2002, obstacles still remain for Mexican truckers driving their rigs in the United States. Federal highway authorities have imposed a series of complicated requirements on Mexican drivers and their trucks, including knowledge of English, which in practice greatly limits the exercise of this right.

10. For further information on some of these ideas, see Robert Pastor, *Toward a North American Community: Lessons from the Old World for the New,* Washington, DC: Institute for International Economics, 2001; the North American Forum on Integration (www.fina-nafi.org); and Wendy Dobson, "Shaping the Future of the North American Economic Space: A Framework for Action," *C.D. Howe Institute Commentary 162 (April 2002).*

11. In the end, the "Smart Border" agreement signed between Canada and the United States at the end of 2001 was very similar to the one signed three months earlier by Mexico and the United States. With the exception of asylum and refugee issues on the one hand, and migration issues on the other, almost all of the problems faced by Canada in the post–September 11 scenario on its border with the United States were similar to those experienced by Mexico on its northern frontier.

12. During the first two years of the Fox administration, the Special Office for Mexicans Abroad was headed by a Mexican-American, Juan Hernández. It was closed in the fall of 2002 and its functions transferred to the Foreign Ministry, which already had a Directorate for Community Affairs. Constant friction between Hernández and the consular network pointed to a considerable duplication in functions and suggested that the high profile Fox intended to convey with this office was more a myth than a reality. Subsequently, Fox launched the Consejo Consultivo del Instituto de los Mexicanos en el Exterior as an advisory body of Mexican-Americans to help define the government's agenda. This too has proved to be a source of conflict among the various groups in the United States that claim to represent the Mexican community's interests.

13. In 1946, Mexico was chosen by lottery for a one-year term on the first Security Council. In 1980–1981, Mexico was asked by Cuba and Colombia to break the deadlock between them and take the Latin American seat. On both these occasions, Mexico's presence on the Council was for reasons attributable to others.

14. Soon after the Iraq crisis became the most important issue for Washington's foreign policy in late 2002 and early 2003, those Mexican critics who opposed Fox's decision to get Mexico a seat on the Security Council engaged in a loud exercise of "I told you so."

15. *Los Angeles Times,* February 14, 2001.

16. Fox and Aguilar believed that such a position, located in the presidential office, would help coordinate the many aspects of domestic security policy heretofore haphazardly dealt with by various cabinet officers and departments. They seemingly ignored the fact that such a post would inevitably create conflict with the Ministries of the Interior and Defense, as well as with the attorney general. When Fox decided to dismantle the office that had caused constant frictions with the rest of the domestic cabinet, Aguilar was named to head the Mexican Permanent Mission to the UN. It was public knowledge that the foreign minister opposed the appointment and when he was unable to get the president to reverse it, decided to sever all direct contacts with his longtime friend.

17. In an unprecedented move, President Bush is said to have remarked to Fox when they met in Cabo San Lucas on the occasion of the APEC summit: "Mr. President, we have a problem with your ambassador in New York." The personal animosity between Aguilar Zinser and U.S. ambassador John Negroponte was an open secret in the corridors of the UN and there were several occasions of direct hostility between the two New York missions, including a murmured remark by a U.S. press officer waiting to get his ambassador to meet the press outside the Security Council, while Aguilar was in the middle of his press conference, to the effect that "someone should get the Mexican to finish . . . nobody really cares about what he has to say."

18. From the outset of his administration, President Fox and Foreign Minister Castañeda had entrusted the author with several confidential missions related to Mexico's candidacy for the Security Council, relations with Venezuelan president Hugo Chavéz, and the revival of the defunct Group of Three (Mexico, Colombia, and Venezuela) consultative mechanism set up during the Salinas presidency.

19. Mexico's diplomacy has often attempted to offer mediation to the United States and Cuba. As early as 1981, a secret meeting between Secretary of State Alexander Haig and Cuban vice president Carlos Rafael Rodríguez was held in the home of Mexico's then–foreign minister Jorge Castañeda senior. But Washington's responses to Mexican initiatives on Cuba have been met by consistent rebuffs and claims that the United States and Cuba have sufficient direct links and channels of communication so as not to need any third-party assistance.

20. The name commonly given to the Mexican Ministry of Foreign Affairs as a result of its location in the pre-Columbian Tlatelolco area of Mexico City.

21. In order to transfer the existing deputy secretary of international trade negotiations from the Ministry of the Economy to Foreign Affairs, Congress must approve changes to existing laws and regulations. In the meantime, Derbez has continued as de facto head of the trade agenda and has dedicated much of his time in office to attending meetings and negotiations related to trade matters.

22. These terms refer to the two most important books written in the past decades on the U.S.-Mexican relationship: *Distant Neighbors* by Alan Riding (New York: Knopf, 1985), and *Limits to Friendship,* coauthored by Jorge G. Castañeda and Robert Pastor (New York: Knopf, 1988).

5

U.S.-Mexican Relations: A View from Mexico

Luis Carlos Ugalde

From time to time, newly inaugurated administrations in Mexico have tried to shake the foundations of relations with the United States and establish new bases for bilateral foreign policies. Frequently, these attempts are based on grand visions, goodwill, and close relations between chief executives on both sides of the border. In recent years, this has been the case most notably of Carlos Salinas de Gortari (1988–1994) and Vicente Fox (2000–2006), both of whom came into office expecting to alter the terms of the bilateral relationship. The former promised to transform a history of mistrustful neighbors into a partnership for prosperity based on free trade and market-oriented reforms in Mexico that would open new opportunities for investment and business. His audacious moves were helped by a close relationship with George H. W. Bush and his Texan team of probusiness advisers eager to forge trade relations with Mexico.

Vicente Fox offered a "NAFTA plus" vision in which free trade would be enhanced by opening borders to the flow of labor across North America. His strategy was to use what his first foreign minister called his "democratic bonus" as an instrument to gain credibility and trust among Washington players usually skeptical of their Mexican counterparts. Fox's initial overture was supported by his close relationship with George W. Bush and by the democratic aura that momentarily and marginally increased his leverage in Washington politics. However, economic recession, electoral calculations, and the change of priorities in response to the terrorist attacks of September 11 soon took precedence in the United States and have delayed Fox's attempt to open a new era in bilateral relations.

This chapter assesses the impact of democratization in Mexico on bilateral relations with the United States, focusing on the electoral triumph of Vicente Fox and his attempt to reshape migration affairs. Is it accurate to describe the period following Fox's arrival to the presidency as a new era in bilateral relations? Why was a broad migration agreement not yet been reached with the United States, as Fox had promised? Has the new democratic character of the Mexican government in itself acted as a force to alter bilateral relations?

I argue that democratization has affected Mexico's approach toward the United States in four ways. First, democratization has gradually multiplied the number of actors involved in foreign policy decision-making, leading to increased contacts and a faster pace of cooperation on specific issues between subnational actors in both countries. Second, democratization has empowered Mexico's Congress, which today plays an important role in commenting on and assessing the nation's foreign policy, thus constraining the political maneuvers of the executive branch. Third, democratization has amplified the voice of public opinion and has thereby indirectly influenced foreign policy through its impact on presidential approval rates. And fourth, the electoral triumph of Vicente Fox in July 2000 increased the country's democratic legitimacy and altered the perceptions of U.S. policymakers regarding Mexico's credibility, marginally increasing the leverage of Mexico in bilateral negotiations. This allowed new items to be introduced to the agenda and moderated forces usually opposed to changing the status quo in areas such as migration and the fight against drug trafficking.

Although democratization has altered Mexican politics and the perception of Mexico in the United States, it has not led to a significant change in bilateral relations. The simultaneous beginning of two administrations in 2000–2001 in Mexico City and Washington, D.C., as well as the democratic bonus ascribed to Vicente Fox as the first president in modern history not from the PRI, did indeed open a window of opportunity, however small, to make changes in the U.S.-Mexican relationship. Yet, those attempts were rapidly overshadowed by other political, economic, and security factors in the United States. For example, the condition of the U.S. economy, electoral and political interests, the terrorist attacks of September 11, 2001, and the war on Iraq played a greater role in defining the outcome of negotiations between Mexico and the United States than the changes under way within Mexican politics. Even if the attacks had not occurred, the audacious move by the Mexican government to introduce a "NAFTA plus" scheme to liberalize the labor market across North America would have had very limited success.

Cooperation Prior to Democratization

If conflict intermittently permeated the history of U.S.-Mexican relations during the nineteenth century and the first half of the twentieth century, cooperation became more common once Mexico began market-oriented reforms in the mid-1980s. Recent scholarship tends to support the conclusion that increased cooperation was accompanied and reinforced by a gradual process of institutionalization of the bilateral relationship. Institutionalization refers to the construction of norms and organizations to order policy discussions. It provides certainty and continuity and can be measured in terms of clearer rules to deal with issues, new mechanisms to solve conflicts, and committees and working groups to explore alternatives. Institutionalization reduces bargaining and information costs for both governments, which, in turn, facilitates cooperation.[1]

Globalization and the need to implement structural economic reforms in the mid-1980s and early 1990s led the Mexican government and the entrepreneurial sector to build new bridges of cooperation and business interaction with the United States. At the same time, the end of the Cold War facilitated a closer relationship between the United States and Mexico based on issues other than security. Within this context, NAFTA can be seen as a reflection of institutionalized cooperation based on shared interests regarding investment and trade.[2]

Mexico's private sector was the first set of actors to influence collectively the nation's foreign policy and bring it closer to its commercial and business goals. Closer relations with the United States were at the top of this agenda. The new export-led economic model Mexico was beginning to implement gave these groups an impetus to build new channels of communication with their U.S. counterparts.[3] It was during the administration of President Carlos Salinas (1988–1994) that the institutionalization of bilateral relations at the federal level began and was strengthened through the creation of working groups and special commissions. Trade liberalization was the necessary condition for this institutionalization to occur.[4]

However, analysts of the bilateral relationship were intrigued to observe how Mexico's foreign policy toward the United States was becoming more pragmatic in some areas while continuing its attachment to old traditions in others. For example, while the government's economic strategy in the early 1990s favored globalization, privatization, and free trade, its diplomacy continued to emphasize nonintervention, sovereignty, and nationalism.[5] Mexico was turning right on economic policy but continued to veer left in its political diplomacy.

Economic modernization and market reforms in Mexico both required and stimulated renewed cooperation with the United States, as more investment and trade were needed for the model to be successful. More recently, democratization has encouraged, in turn, a realignment of Mexico's traditional diplomatic stance of nationalism, self-determination, and nonintervention toward values of universalism, respect for human rights, and defense of democratic values. As democratization progressed during the 1990s, it became increasingly difficult for the Mexican government to hold strictly to its principles and reject, for example, the participation of foreign observers in Mexican elections. Lack of flexibility would have only increased suspicions about the cleanliness of the electoral system and prompted international criticism. The Zapatista movement, which erupted in 1994, brought international attention to the violation of human rights in Mexico and helped introduce international NGOs as new players in Mexico's domestic politics. As the political opening continued, Mexican officials discovered that it was better to talk, lobby, and try to counterbalance international criticisms than simply reject the idea of others expressing their views of Mexico's domestic affairs.

As Guadalupe González has written, "Increased domestic pressures for democratization since 1994 and the proliferation of governance problems—guerrilla groups, political assassinations and the consolidation of organized crime—have compelled the Mexican government to accept the participation of international institutions and foreign actors in some aspects of Mexico's democratization process. . . . Mexican foreign policy has moved away from ideology to pragmatism."[6] (In light of Mexico's decision to oppose the U.S. war on Iraq even in the face of expected costs in its relationship with the Bush administration, many may question whether Mexico has indeed shifted from ideology to pragmatism, or whether it is returning to its principled positions.)

To summarize, market reforms in Mexico and economic integration with the United States stimulated greater cooperation between both countries long before democracy fully arrived in Mexico. Democratization has strengthened the realignment of Mexico's noninterventionist foreign policy toward one based more on strategic interests. Institutionalization of the bilateral relationship was only a means to order and channel increased transactions arising from this new framework.

The Impact of Democratization on Foreign Policy Decisionmaking

Democratization has played a role in changing the structure of the U.S.-Mexican decisionmaking process. Actors involved in foreign policy–making have multiplied, and bilateral decisions are no longer the monopoly of the foreign secretary in Mexico City. In the old days of PRI predominance, the executive branch was almost exclusively responsible for Mexico's foreign policy. Opposition at home was minimal, as few independent voices existed, and the president had ample leeway to conduct relations with the United States as he saw fit. The most significant new actor to appear as a result of democratization is Congress, an old player with new power.[7] As will be seen in the following section, the legislative branch has become an influential voice in matters of foreign policy toward the United States.

Democratization has also played a key role in multiplying state-level actors in areas previously dominated by the Secretary of Foreign Relations. This phenomenon is particularly evident among state governments, especially those that have experienced alternation in party control over the past few years. Alternation at the state level began in 1989 with the first gubernatorial triumph of an opposition party in modern Mexican history—the victory of the rightist PAN in Baja California in 1989. Since then, there have been about eighteen changes in party affiliation at the state level of government, either from PRI to PAN or PRD rule, or vice versa. (See Table 5.1.)

Alternation in state governments during the 1990s resulted in many governors carrying out their own bilateral negotiations with their counterparts in the United States, especially in trade, investment, tourism, and cultural exchange. Many of these leaders were members of opposition parties and were naturally distrustful of the central government. This was true not only for border states economically tied to the United States, but also for states in central and southern Mexico. As the 1990s progressed, state governments representing both the PRI and the opposition parties began to open offices in the United States to promote investment and tourism and to deal with migrants living in the United States. State governments have discovered the benefits of having their own diplomatic apparatus at home to deal with actors in the United States, instead of relying on Mexico City.

During the 1990s, non-PRI governors were reluctant to request support from the Secretary of Foreign Relations, which was headed by PRI supporters. Since 2000, the reverse has been true, with PRI governors feeling compelled to act more independently of a federal government headed by the PAN. This increased autonomy on foreign policy at the state level does not imply a clash with Mexico City over decision-making or its implementation, but rather a natural distrust arising from the first experience of alternation in the presidency. Table 5.1 shows the dramatic increase in the number of state governments representing a different party than the one in power at the federal level, a phenomenon known as "juxtaposed government" that intensified as many PRI governments moved into the opposition with the presidential triumph of Vicente Fox in 2000.

As state actors multiplied, so did nongovernmental actors. Business associations, lobbying groups, and firms on both sides of the border have been involved in promoting faster integration than would have been possible under the sole intervention of government officials. NGOs have stimulated the emergence of transnational alliances to promote human rights, civic education, gender equality, and the promotion of democracy. Unions and labor organizations in Mexico and the United States, which until a few years ago had no direct relationship, have begun bilateral contacts to promote shared interests in the region.[8]

The greater number of actors brought about by democratization, as well as the decentralization of the decisionmaking process caused by the emergence of state governors as diplomatic envoys, has increased the channels of communication and bargaining among players on both sides of the border. As more actors and contact points exist within a framework of greater economic and trade integration, cooperation has tended to increase.

The Mexican Congress: Old Player, New Power

During the old days of hegemonic PRI rule, Mexico's presidents were powerful enough to make bilateral commitments to the United States

Table 5.1 Democratization at the State Level, 1989–2003
        (selected years)

Year	Number of Alternations in State Governments	Number of Juxtaposed Governments
1989	1	1
1991	0	1
1992	1	2
1994	0	2
1995	2	4
1996	0	4
1997	3	7
1998	4	9
1999	1	10
2000	3	23
2001	1	22
2002	0	22
2003	2	22
Total	18	

Source: http://www.cidac.org.

without first consulting Congress, which was also dominated by the PRI and over which the presidency exerted enormous influence and control.[9] Mexican negotiators were effective in Washington because they could always deliver on their promises even if it meant imposing their decisions on Congress. Consequently, bilateral cooperation with Mexico was relatively expeditious and easy to attain.

One consequence of democratization in Mexico is the experience of divided government that began in 1997 when the PRI lost its majority in the Chamber of Deputies for the first time since the party was founded in 1929. Although divided government can be seen as a reflection of a democratic Mexico capable of being a trusted partner in international diplomacy, it also means that Mexico's chief executive is subject to new constraints. Democracy in Mexico, widely lauded in Washington, may come at the expense of a Mexico that is less predictable and less able to deliver on its promises.

Once democracy arrived and Congress gained a voice in foreign policy, bargaining became a necessary condition for the chief executive, first to commit to a policy and then to deliver on it. As scholars who have modeled this type of negotiation and ratification process point out, any chief negotiator at the international level needs to have a domestic support base in order to get agreements ratified by a coalition that usually involves the legislative branch.[10] In countries characterized by authoritarian rule, like Mexico before the 1990s, the ratification process is meaningless since the president has ample power to influence and obtain ratification from domestic actors even when they do not agree with him or participate at the bargaining table.

In Mexico, democratization has empowered the domestic actors needed to ratify deals reached at the international level, even though Congress's influence is still limited in matters of foreign policy.[11] Nevertheless, Congress is playing a greater role in constraining the drafting and implementation of Mexico's foreign policy. Other scholars argue that, far from weakening the role played by the president on the international scene, the need to obtain ratification from domestic constituencies actually strengthens the hand of the Mexican president in negotiations with the United States because he can demand the greater concessions needed to secure ratification. Divided government at home, therefore, may fortify rather than diminish Mexico's position vis-à-vis the United States. Yet, government officials tend to accuse Congress of weakening Mexico's position abroad. For example, former president Salinas used to argue during NAFTA negotiations that opposition at home, usually from leftist parties such as the PRD, only reduced Mexico's bargaining power. In reality, opposition at home might have had precisely the reverse effect in President Salinas's negotiations with the United States.

More recently, Congress has been accused of obstructing Mexico's foreign policy on a variety of issues. Critics point to the delay in ratifying the Rome Statute of the International Criminal Court in 2002, the Senate's denial of Fox's request to travel to the United States and Canada in mid-2002, and fierce criticism of the administration's new policy toward Cuba, as evidence of congressional obstructionism.[12] Empirical evidence, however, suggests otherwise. Of the twenty-four permits requested by the president to travel abroad in the 2000–2002 period, only the one referred to above was rejected. One hundred and nine of the president's diplomatic appointments have been ratified by the Senate, with only two facing opposition and delays in Congress—and in both cases the appointments were eventually approved.[13] These numbers show that despite rhetorical and political antagonisms, the legislative branch played a cooperative rather than an obstructionist role during the first two years of President Fox's administration. Cooperation was, however, accompanied by a more outspoken Congress whose political positions sometimes contradicted those of the administration and did constrain the president's role as chief diplomatic officer.

Democratization and Public Opinion

To understand why the Mexican Congress is traditionally distrustful of closer ties with Washington, it is necessary to consider public opinion, which has become an influential factor shaping congressional behavior. For the past century, the Mexican people had a love/hate attitude toward the United States. This is not unusual for small countries that share borders with large countries, and where huge economic and military asymmetries have led the more powerful state to try to colonize or dominate the weaker. Relations between Mexico and the United States fit such a pattern. Anti-U.S. sentiment was a natural response to expansionist U.S. policies that led to the loss of half of Mexico's territory in 1848 and a series of military and political interventions in the following decades, most notably the occupation by U.S. troops of the port of Veracruz in 1914. These feelings were reinforced by successive Mexican governments that used anti-Americanism as a diplomatic and political instrument to protect the country from U.S. interventionism, legitimize their "revolutionary origins," offset popular discontent with the government, and keep themselves in power.

Hostile sentiments and anti-Americanism have waned steadily over the past two decades, although the war on Iraq reversed those tendencies, at least temporarily. In October 2001, for example, 54 percent of Mexicans had warm feelings of *simpatía* toward the United States, with only 19 percent manifesting more negative feelings. After the Iraq war, warm feelings plummeted to only 34 percent in late March 2003 and hostile sentiments jumped to 28 percent.[14] The Fox administration's decision not to support President George W. Bush's action against Iraq (discussed in more detail below) can be partially explained by the shape of public opinion. (See Table 5.2.)

On issues other than war, however, many Mexicans now have a more pragmatic and nonideological attitude. For them, prospects for employment north of the border, as well as trade and economic interactions, have created new opportunities for Mexicans. Today, 78 percent of the population believes Mexico's interests are closer to those of the United States than to Latin America, and 52 percent identify Mexico's national interest as being best served by greater collaboration with its northern neighbor. Only 34 percent believe Mexico should highlight its differences and maintain its distance from the United States.[15]

As more Mexicans develop personal contacts with the United States, either directly through travel or work, or indirectly through family living abroad, traditional *antiyanqui* stereotypes have changed. In the eyes of many, the United States is becoming a land of opportunity rather than a land of domination or imperialism. This explains why a majority of Mexicans consider the United States to be their most important ally.

While the Mexican population has adopted a more pragmatic attitude toward the United States, some political elites retain a more ideological stance based in part on the mistaken belief that Mexicans continue to be

Table 5.2 Sentiments Toward the United States: People's Perceptions (in percentages)

	October 2001	February 18, 2003	War Begins March 19–21, 2003	March 27, 2003	April 8, 2003
Hate	19.0	15.3		28.0	25.2
Sympathy	54.2	50.2		34.0	37.4
Do not know	26.8	34.5		38.0	37.4
Total	100.0	100.0		100.0	100.0

Source: Consulta Mitofsky (www.consulta.com.mx).

highly anti-U.S. Most of those political leaders who distrust the United States belong to leftist parties and to the traditionalist wing of the PRI. Their beliefs were crafted by public school education that reinforced the nationalistic rhetoric of the postrevolutionary years. The gap between the beliefs of some Mexican lawmakers and those of the population at large continues to be an obstacle to forging closer relations with the United States. Anti-U.S. elites argue that Washington dismisses the importance of Mexico as a worthy partner and cite the Bush administration's recent neglect of its southern neighbor as proof that a more submissive attitude on the part of Mexico toward the United States does not necessarily lead to gains. For Mexican members of Congress to realign their views more closely with those of their constituencies, they must be convinced that it will pay politically to be friendlier with Washington. Unfortunately, the Bush administration's post–September 11 indifference, despite efforts on the part of the Fox administration to gain its attention, only fuels the idea that distance rather than dialogue is the best strategy for getting respect from U.S. politicians.

Mexican elites, however, fail to acknowledge that the apparent indifference of the Bush administration may have been fueled in part by a lack of solidarity and political support from the Mexican government in the aftermath of the terrorist attacks. When President Fox made a state visit to Washington just days before September 11, Mexican officials and lawmakers were eager to laud the benefits of closer relations with the United States. After the attacks, however, some of those officials opted to keep silent and were ambiguous in showing their full support to the U.S. government. Some other leftist politicians and intellectuals even implicitly justified the terrorist attacks as punishment for U.S. imperialism in the Middle East. If the imperialistic demeanor of the United States has long created distrust among Mexicans regarding closer relations with their neighbor, Mexico's *antiyanqui* positions, especially in times of human tragedy, have not helped either.

The Democratic Bonus and
Its Impact on Migration Negotiations

Vicente Fox's electoral triumph had its greatest impact on the bilateral relationship in the area of migration. The debate over migration ignited by Fox as soon as he was elected president was intense and controversial, but soon languished when other political and economic factors and unexpected events claimed the attention of U.S. politicians. The high hopes created when President Bush declared that Mexico and Latin

America would become Washington priorities were soon overshadowed by lack of progress after September 11.

As president-elect, Fox had visited Washington in August 2000 and proposed a "NAFTA plus" scheme that included not only the free movement of products and services across borders, but also of labor. He said he had in mind the European Union model in which advanced economies helped backward nations such as Portugal and Spain converge economically and become part of the union. He imagined a process of economic convergence that would allow Mexico to meet targets on inflation, interest rates, and other criteria, and simultaneously receive financial assistance from its northern neighbors to narrow the economic gap that separates it from the United States and Canada. He reiterated that if the European Union had achieved integration by including less-developed nations, so could North America.[16]

After his stop in Washington, Fox visited then-candidate George W. Bush in his home state of Texas. The Republican showed openness and warmth toward Fox's ideas, leading many to believe that the time had come for profound changes on the migration front, provided Bush won. In Washington, U.S. officials privately expressed mixed feelings toward Fox's NAFTA expansion proposal, especially regarding the opening of labor markets given the huge wage differential between the two countries.[17] Fox may have been perceived as utopian by trying to emulate the European Community's free flow of goods, services, and labor, but the democratic credentials he enjoyed for having ousted the long-ruling PRI created a natural sympathy for his ideas even if they lacked viability or coherence. Nobody in Washington wanted to express doubts or openly contradict the proposals, however unworkable, of the man perceived as the first truly democratic Mexican president in modern times.

Six months after that first visit to Washington and Texas, and once both men had been inaugurated as presidents of their respective countries, Bush visited Mexico in February 2001 and met President Fox at his ranch in the state of Guanajuato. Fox's ideas had evolved; he had left behind his aspirations for a North American version of the European Union and had more specific and limited proposals in mind. Fox took the opportunity to push his migration proposal and suggested that some sort of amnesty or regularization for millions of illegal Mexicans working in the United States should be on the agenda. Although the White House expressed doubts that amnesty was the means to deal with the issue, as many considered it a way to reward illegal behavior and increase, rather than diminish, the future flow of illegal migrants, President Bush himself showed respect for the bold proposal of his Mexican counterpart.

Despite doubts over the Fox proposals, agreement was reached at the Guanajuato meeting to create a binational immigration working group headed by the secretary of state and the attorney general on the U.S. side, and by the secretary of the interior and the secretary of foreign relations on the Mexican side. The group had the official mandate of discussing ways to "develop an orderly framework for migration that ensures humane treatment, legal security and dignified labor conditions." In early April 2001, the working group defined an agenda that included five elements: regularization, a guest-worker program, a special regime for granting more visas to Mexican workers, security for and humane treatment of Mexican migrants, and economic development as a means of reducing incentives for migration.[18]

The Fox government never mentioned targets for the number of undocumented Mexicans it expected to be regularized, nor did it discuss how large a guest-worker program might be. However, it is important to have some sense of the numbers involved. According to the U.S. Census Bureau, in July 2001 there were 37 million Latinos in the United States. If 60 percent of that figure is assumed to be of Mexican origin, it is likely that 22.2 million of these immigrants are of Mexican origin, including both legal and illegal.[19] According to the census, out of that figure, about 8.7 million were born in Mexico and arrived in the United States after 1990. Of that, about 4.5–4.7 million Mexicans are thought to be undocumented, making up 55 percent of all illegal immigrants in the United States.[20]

How many of those 4.5–4.7 million undocumented Mexicans could have applied for regularization? According to the Pew Hispanic Center, the answer depends on how many years of residence would be required before applying for regularization. If the mark were set at ten years, about 2.3 million would be eligible. If the prerequisite were five years, about 3.4 million could apply.[21] As for the guest-worker program, the potential numbers involved would depend on how many undocumented workers are currently employed or needed in key sectors of the U.S. economy. The Pew Hispanic Center estimated that "more than a million undocumented persons are employed in manufacturing and a similar number in the service industry. More than 600,000 work in construction and more than 700,000 in restaurants." Between 1 million and 1.4 million unauthorized workers, about half of them Mexican, are employed in U.S. agriculture.[22] Taken together, Fox's proposals concerning regularization and a guest-worker program would potentially have encompassed between 3 million and 4 million workers.

A few weeks after the Guanajuato meeting, some members of the Bush administration began signaling privately that migration talks would need to proceed slowly. According to diplomatic sources, the U.S. ambassador to Mexico from 1998 to 2002, Jeffrey Davidow, delivered a message to the Fox administration in August 2002 suggesting a partial approach. The idea was to proceed first with a guest-worker program, something that was politically feasible at the time, and leave regularization for a more propitious second stage. The Mexican government, led by Foreign Minister Jorge Castañeda, rejected the idea, convinced that a partial victory on one of the fronts would reduce the viability of the rest of the proposal. For Mexico, regularization was the key element of the migration accord.

It is important to mention the changing role of the U.S. labor movement, particularly the AFL-CIO, in shaping support for Fox's migration initiative. In the early 1990s, as a means of protecting the jobs of U.S. workers, trade unions had opposed any proposal to legalize undocumented workers. However, after several years of steady economic growth during the late 1990s, during which neither NAFTA nor immigration flows threatened U.S. jobs, and in response to a declining union membership that was reducing the electoral power of the labor movement, the AFL-CIO realized it would be politically wise to change its strategy and find more flexible positions regarding immigration. By engaging in contacts with Mexican unions, the AFL-CIO sought to build transnational alliances that, in turn, could encourage Mexican workers in the United States to become members of the federation.

The AFL-CIO, as well as the Mexican-American community, had both been supportive of Fox's proposal to put regularization on the table, but they were against a guest-worker program as it did not favor their political interests. These groups made clear that if the Mexican government opted to proceed first with a guest-worker program, they would oppose the whole negotiation. Suddenly, the Fox administration was at risk of losing key allies in its efforts to alter migration policies. To prevent the partial approach suggested by Washington, Foreign Minister Castañeda insisted on a maximalist approach, which, in a now famous sound byte, he called the "whole enchilada." Castañeda used this colloquial expression to signal that either the package had to be considered as a whole—regularization and a guest-worker program— or nothing would be acceptable to Mexico. This strategy was thought to be the only means available to avoid tipping the scales toward U.S. interests and still guarantee achievements in migrant regularization.[23]

Despite different approaches that were gradually emerging over the pace and content of the migration accord, President Fox's state visit to Washington in early September 2001, just days before the terrorist attacks of September 11, marked the high point of the brief but intense honeymoon between the two administrations. Before departing for Washington, Fox restated his grand vision for U.S.-Mexican relations in an opinion column published in the *New York Times:*

> Addressing the situation of more than three million Mexicans currently in the United States without legal status is one of the central issues in the negotiations currently underway between our governments, along with significant increases in legal entries, a seasonal or guest worker program, and even a shared border-control program. . . . Working and living conditions would improve for Mexican workers in the United States, disincentives would be created for workers crossing the border without documents and, with the right regional development programs, the Mexican work force could be given economic incentives to stay home, bringing about growth in my country.[24]

Fox sounded a moderate note when he declared it would take "four to six years to complete a comprehensive U.S.-Mexico immigration reform, including legalization for some undocumented Mexican workers in the United States."[25] However, just three days after he admitted that his proposal would require years to complete, Fox abruptly changed his mind. During the welcoming ceremony at the White House he said that the migration agreement would need to be completed by year's end, that is to say, only four months later. Fox's remarks were described in the *Washington Post* as an "unwelcome surprise" to the administration, while other newspapers noted that they had caught the White House off-guard, especially in light of the earlier comments. According to sources closely involved with the visit, the unexpected decision by President Fox to establish a deadline was made in Washington just hours before the ceremony and had been conveyed to U.S. officials the previous night. By all accounts, it was Foreign Minister Jorge Castañeda who had persuaded Fox to change the migration bargaining timetable, arguing it was necessary to catch U.S. politicians off-guard in order for the migration proposal to gain momentum and increase the chances that it would succeed at the bargaining table.

Bush politely abstained from commenting on the Fox deadline. Calling for an honest assessment of reality, he expressed hope that a route to legalization could be created for some of the more than 3 million undocumented Mexicans living in the United States, but he also made it clear that an amnesty was out of the question. U.S. lawmakers were divided. House Democratic Leader Richard Gephardt, for example, said that he agreed with Fox's request for quick action on immigration and thought that legislation was possible by the end of the year. Others, like Representative Tom Tancredo, a Colorado Republican, opposed any amnesty for illegal immigrants.

In general, Democrats tended to support regularization of undocumented workers, while Republicans were more prone to favor a guest-worker program, with their positions reflecting the traditional core of both parties. Democrats favored regularization in the belief that new documented workers would affiliate with unions close to their party and strengthen the declining membership of the AFL-CIO. Republicans supported a guest-worker program to fill labor shortages and keep wages down in the farm, agribusiness, and packing industries. For the Mexican government, the fact that Republican and Democratic votes would both be needed to pass a broad migration accord supported the "whole enchilada" approach suggested by Castañeda. Otherwise, legislators on either side of the aisle could block a partial agreement if their half of the "enchilada" were not included in the package.

Despite partisan differences, President Fox's message during his visit to Washington was received respectfully, a response that probably had more to do with the feelings legislators had for Fox personally than with the content or viability of his ideas. Legislators from both parties gave the president a warm reception when he addressed a joint session of Congress, an unusual honor. According to the *New York Times,* Fox used his personal and democratic legitimacy to "help level the playing field in negotiations with the United States over contentious issues like narcotics trafficking and illegal immigration. He also hopes to turn the burgeoning feelings of trust between Washington and Mexico City into reforms and programs that will help lift his nation out of social distress."[26]

Building on the power of his democratic bonus, Vicente Fox had crafted a well-designed speech based on the idea of trust as a means to achieve cooperation. The underlying argument was that democracy had produced a transparent and credible government in Mexico that could help overcome distrust and promote new avenues for cooperation between Mexico and the United States. "Simple trust, that is what has been sorely absent in our relationship in the past, and that is what is required for us to propel and strengthen our relationship in the days and weeks and years to come," said Fox. "Only trust will allow us to constructively tackle the challenges our two nations face as we undertake building a new partnership in North America. . . . Thanks to those democratic changes inaugurated in Mexico last year on July the 2nd, the time has come for Mexico and the United States to trust each other." He concluded: "Members of this Congress, give trust a chance."[27]

Fox was convinced that his legitimacy was the key weapon to make a difference in Washington politics. He returned to Mexico full of optimism despite signals that the White House wanted to proceed cautiously. Most commentators agreed the visit had been a complete success. Lacking inside knowledge from Washington, many political observers thought

Mexico was on its way to producing a significant change in its relationship with the United States.

The September 11 Attacks
and the Erosion of the Democratic Bonus

Four days after Fox left the U.S. capital, the terrorist attacks on targets
in New York and Washington ended the honeymoon Mexico had
enjoyed with the United States for almost a year. Since then, the migration agenda has been frozen despite several efforts on the part of the
Mexican government to relaunch discussions. The democratic bonus
that had helped Fox put migration on the negotiating table had come to
an end.[28]

The first formal attempt to resume migration talks came when Fox
met President Bush during the International Conference on Financing
for Development held in Monterrey under the auspices of the United
Nations in March 2002. There were no positive signs from the U.S.
side. A new opportunity came in October 2002 during the Asia Pacific
Economic Cooperation (APEC) meeting in Los Cabos, Baja California.
President Fox tried to use the summit to get a commitment from Bush
to take up the migration agenda again. However, President Bush's sole
purpose at the time was to get support from Mexico and other members
of the UN Security Council for his proposed resolution to disarm Iraq
by force. Bush left the summit, however, without a pledge from Mexico
to support the U.S. position, and President Fox made it clear Mexico
would side with those countries willing to authorize the use of force
only when Iraq failed to comply with weapons inspections. Many newspapers reported the discomfort Bush felt when Mexico announced it
would abstain from supporting his plea for military action; some observers viewed the abstention as the reason for Washington's disregard
of President Fox's request to resume talks on migration.[29]

Hope persisted and President Fox again issued a public challenge to
the Bush administration to resume talks on migration during the annual
meeting of the cabinet-level binational commission in Mexico City in
November 2002.[30] The U.S. delegation responded quietly and with
reservations. In a taped message to the meeting, President Bush made
no specific commitment to Mexico and requested "patience."

The 2002 midterm elections in the United States only reinforced the
unresolved status of the migration agenda as the U.S. electorate affirmed
its support for Republicans who had focused primarily on security and
the antiterrorist agenda. The election results further diminished the

chances that Congress would push forward a migration agenda whose electoral returns seemed almost nil. As Samuel Aguilar, a PRI legislator, noted after the election, "the fact that Bush has a congressional majority implies a ratification of his militaristic policy and his international agenda in which the issue of the Mexican immigration is shoved to the back burner."[31]

The clearest sign that hopes of obtaining a migration accord needed to be put to rest came in January 2003 when Mexican foreign secretary Jorge Castañeda resigned, blaming frustration over the stalled talks with the United States. The resignation marked a recognition that the initiative would not be viable for years to come. White House spokesman Ari Fleisher announced that the administration regretted Castañeda's departure and admitted that a migration accord with Mexico had slipped further away, as Washington was becoming more preoccupied with Iraq and North Korea. The departure of Castañeda symbolized the end of the most recent attempt on the part of Mexico to change the foundations of the bilateral agenda. It concluded a chapter in which Mexican officials, headed by Fox and Castañeda, truly believed that they, as representatives of a newly democratic Mexico, could create a new symmetry between the two countries. No one will ever know how close Mexico may have come to reaching a broad migration agreement if September 11 had not occurred. However, Ambassador Jeffrey Davidow remarked just after leaving his post that it had been a mistake on the part of the Mexican administration to have bet so much on a single issue, especially one that was so politically unviable. He also pointed out that negotiations within the immigration working group were facing trouble even before the terrorist attacks. The inference is that, even in the absence of September 11, Fox's migration policy package was an illusion.

The War on Iraq:
Democratization and Noncooperation

If democratization at home provided Fox with an aura that enhanced his ability to introduce migration to the negotiating table, democratic forces in Mexico also explain how a diplomatic honeymoon almost became a diplomatic confrontation between Mexico and the United States. The reluctance of the Fox administration to support the U.S. war on Iraq in early 2003 could have converted the already frozen bilateral agenda after September 11 into one of animosity or even confrontation.

In 2001, the Fox administration had sought a seat on the UN Security Council, arguing the time had come for Mexico to be more active in international affairs. The Mexican strategy of avoiding open conflict with the United States on issues beyond the bilateral agenda during the Cold War, as well as the traditional principle of noninterventionism that had kept Mexico silent in many international conflicts, had to give way, in the views of Fox and Castañeda, to a foreign policy more active in defending human rights and democracy around the world. Mexico's new democracy provided the country and its government with the legitimacy to act internationally as it had not done in the past. Using this political rationale, Mexico lobbied for and received a seat on the Security Council. However, the Fox administration did not anticipate the way world politics would evolve as a result of September 11 and the risk it would face in confronting Washington.

When the United States began campaigning in late 2002 to get support from the United Nations to disarm Iraq by force, Mexico sided with Russia and France in their attempt to give more time to the Iraqi regime and avoid the use of force. Sentiment in Mexico was divided. On the one hand, public opinion and Congress supported Fox's position against the use of force and condemned Bush's militaristic goals. On the other hand, some opinion leaders cautioned against the dangers such a position could imply for Mexico on matters related to migration, border management, and even trade. If war was not to be deterred by a Mexican vote, then why should Mexico embark on such an adventure, risking the interests of millions of Mexican migrants on U.S. soil who could suffer the consequences of a more stringent migration policy? Why had Mexico sought to be a member of the Security Council in the first place if such a move implied potential frictions with Washington?

Despite internal controversies, the Fox administration, gauging the benefits and costs of aligning either with Washington or with domestic public opinion, opted to respond to the majority of Mexicans who were against the war. In opposing Washington, Fox also increased his approval rating at home. Most pollsters agreed at the time that the upsurge in Fox's popularity, which jumped about ten points in the weeks following the war on Iraq (April and May 2003), is partly explained by his position not to support Washington (see Table 5.3).

It was indeed the first time since Fox was inaugurated that he received an almost unanimous chorus of support from public opinion, the media, and Congress. Leftist parties and the PRI, which had criticized Fox incessantly for almost any endeavor he embarked upon, stood behind the president and supported his decision.

Was the Fox administration's decision not to support Washington the result of electoral calculation, or was it a moral decision based on the principle of noninterventionism? Was Mexico taking revenge for the

Table 5.3 Presidential Approval Rates, 2001–2003 (in percentages)

	February 2001	August 2001	February 2002	August 2002	February 2003	May 2003
Approve	69.7	61.6	44.6	56.7	53.2	63.5
Disapprove	22.9	32.2	53.1	38.0	43.4	33.7

Source: Consulta Mitofsky (www.consulta.com.mx), "Décima evaluación de gobierno del presidente Fox," May 2003.

Bush administration's neglect of its interests since September 11, or was it acting because of political constraints at home? The motivations behind President Fox's position will never be known, but they seem to encompass both political calculations and domestic constraints. If outcomes can say something about the motivations behind a decision, then the upsurge in the president's popularity supports the belief that he acted with an eye on polls. Had he decided to support Washington in the face of public opposition at home, his popularity would have suffered as much as his party's electoral prospects did in the 2003 midterm elections.[32] Foreign policy decisionmaking partly constrained by electoral considerations is one of the latest developments of Mexico's competitive party democracy. This scenario is completely different from what it would have been a decade earlier when public opinion in Mexico mattered little for bilateral relations.

U.S. Constraints on Cooperation

Mexican government officials and many commentators have explained the lack of results of President Fox's strategy on migration as a result of the September 11 attacks. If only days before the terrorist attacks President Fox had made a successful state visit to Washington and received a warm reception from a crowded joint session of Congress, the argument goes, then the terrorist attacks became the most visible obstacle to reaching an agreement on migration.

However, an alternative argument can be offered: even if September 11 had not occurred, an agreement on migration along the lines proposed by Fox was unlikely, given domestic constraints in the United States. When Bush and Fox appointed the binational immigration working group, the Mexican president expected it to yield initial results by the end of the summer of 2001. Yet, according to the *New York Times,* in August 2001 the Bush administration, "daunted by the resistance to the working group's trial balloons, let the Mexicans know that the White House had decided to move slowly." Former ambassador Davidow's farewell remarks lend credibility to this conjecture.[33]

Experience over the past few years suggests that in order to make profound changes in the bilateral relationship, two conditions are necessary. First, structural factors, such as political and electoral interests, the state of the economy, and demographic tendencies, need to be aligned in favor of the proposed change. Second, there must be facilitating conditions in place that trigger negotiations between administrations and that can create political support for the proposed change. It seems that the migration agenda Fox proposed had plenty of facilitating conditions on its side, most notably the trust and democratic bonus his government enjoyed in Washington, as well as the simultaneous beginning of two administrations whose presidents were very much alike and who enjoyed personal chemistry. However, as the following discussion illustrates, structural factors on the U.S. side were absent or even negative.

Electoral Interests

As the Latino population expanded, reaching 13 percent of the population in the 1990s, and even more in states like California, Illinois, and Texas, politicians began to devise strategies to capture the loyalty of that segment of society. Democrats have traditionally been strong among Latino voters, but Bush's successful attraction of Texan Latinos to support his bids for governor in the 1990s showed that Republicans could exert influence among this segment of the electorate. A common belief emerged in both parties that to attract Latino voters required certain actions to support policies demanded by their home countries, most notably Mexico. This conviction was probably based on observations of the effectiveness of the Jewish lobby in Washington with regard to Israel. The argument also assumed that an alignment existed between the interests of Latinos in their home countries and those of Latinos living in the United States.

Republicans, and President Bush in particular, will need the Latino vote if they want to be reelected in 2004, especially given the slim margin by which the 2000 election was decided. However, the 2002 midterm elections weakened the causal argument outlined above by showing that Latinos voted for parties based not on how much they supported the needs and demands of their home countries, but rather on opportunities offered to them in the United States, such as education and healthcare. Therefore, the electoral return for supporting a migration accord with Mexico is low for Republicans. This is compounded if one considers how much alienation might be created among certain conservative segments of U.S. society that vote Republican and radically oppose higher quotas for migrants. Moreover, some recent data show that Latinos already living in the United States may prefer to stop illegal flows from Mexico, as more immigrants create strains and anti-immigration sentiments.

The State of the Economy

Evidence suggests that antimigrant sentiments in the United States follow the economic cycle. In boom times, critics of migration tend to diminish, as work opportunities exist for everyone. In contrast, during times of recession, unemployment and social distress create a hostile environment for immigration of any sort. Even before President Fox made his proposal in 2000, the U.S. economy was entering a recessionary cycle, which only worsened after September 11. The U.S. recession can be seen as an additional structural factor that has played a role in blocking a broad migration accord.

Institutional Incapacity

Observers have noted that the chief agency for dealing with migration, the Immigration and Naturalization Service, "lacks the personnel and resources to undertake major programs to regularize either the flow of migrants . . . or the status of millions of undocumented Mexicans inside the United States."[34] Institutional incapacity may be so great that, even if a deal had been reached, it simply would have been impossible to process applications to regularize the status of millions of Mexicans. In this case, "practicality joins politics to suggest that this is not the hour for a comprehensive agreement on migration."[35]

Conclusion

Even before democracy was a reality in Mexico, trade and economic interests on both sides of the border had begun to alter the nature and pace of bilateral cooperation. The United States had long been a suspect partner in the eyes of Mexican politicians as a result of a history of mistrust and even military confrontation; however, in the early 1990s, trade and investment opportunities changed perceptions in Mexico and the United States and stimulated cooperation rather than confrontation. NAFTA was the reflection of a relationship based on shared interests rather than mutual recriminations.

Once economic modernization had taken hold and democratization was in the making in Mexico, a two-part effect took place. Cooperation increased, as more political actors became involved in dealing with bilateral relations. However, democratization also empowered actors previously in the shadows whose interests had not always coincided with those of the United States. The Mexican Congress warrants special attention as an old player with new power, and one whose positions have sometimes constrained, rather than enhanced, bilateral cooperation.

Migration offers a good case for assessing the impact of democratization in Mexico on bilateral relations. On the one hand, Fox's democratic credentials empowered his administration to ignite a debate over migration on terms unheard-of in the past that tipped the scales in favor of Mexico. On the other hand, this democratic aura passed as soon as constraining factors appeared on the U.S. scene, some as a result of September 11 and others that would have blocked a migration deal even if the terrorist attacks had not occurred.

If a migration accord was unlikely even in the absence of September 11, then an important question is whether the Fox administration made a mistake in betting so much on this one issue and creating such high expectations in Mexico. On the one hand, President Fox was audacious in using his legitimacy, which could last only briefly, as a means of reshaping perceptions in Washington and making progress in some areas. No one can contest the fact that the Mexican administration made a conceptual breakthrough regarding how migration is debated and the type of solutions that are needed. In future negotiations, migration talks will have to embody both a stricter law enforcement apparatus at the border, as the United States usually advocates, as well as a discussion of regularization and temporary workers' permits. Even if no accord is reached in the short run, the terms of the debate have been transformed forever and Mexico will enter future negotiations in a more advantageous position.

On the other hand, some critics argue that a few errors in judgment were made along the way. First, it might have been a mistake to believe that a good personal relationship between chief executives could be transformed into a connection strong enough to change the structural factors that shape bilateral relations. Today, there is increasing frustration among Mexican decisionmakers and opinion leaders over the lack of progress in the relationship with the United States. That sentiment has backfired against the administration, with President Fox being accused of having trusted Washington too much and having achieved too little in exchange.

Second, some observers argue Foreign Secretary Castañeda was mistaken in pursuing a maximalist strategy instead of a piecemeal negotiation. Luis Ernesto Derbez, the former secretary of the economy who replaced

Castañeda in February 2003, has criticized his approach and suggested that gradualism is more realistic than the package deal his predecessor had promised. Third, if a comprehensive migration deal was unreachable even before September 11, as available evidence suggests, then the main contours of Fox's foreign relations with the United States during the first two years of his term seem to have been based on wishful thinking rather than on realistic assumptions.

Finally, many diplomats have criticized the way decisions were made inside the Mexican government during the migration negotiations. The enormous influence Castañeda exerted over Fox had the advantage of speeding up decisions that might otherwise have been delayed, but the opportunities for hasty decisions were also increased in the process. If Fox's arrival to power had an impact on bilateral relations as a result of his democratic credentials, his in-house decisionmaking style was rather closed, however audacious it might have been.

Looking to the future, the challenge for the Fox administration is to devise creative ways to speed the pace and broaden the content of the bilateral relationship. Luis Ernesto Derbez faces the daunting task of reinventing U.S.-Mexican relations after the Iraqi war. So far, he has stressed security and border management issues as his priorities, while suggesting a partial approach on migration. Others within the administration have continued to argue that a migration deal is both necessary and possible, either because they are unfamiliar with U.S. politics or simply to gain the support of migrants.

On the U.S. side, some voices have suggested that Mexico should be willing to open up its energy sector if it wants an amnesty deal in exchange. For example, Representative Cass Ballenger (R-N.C.) sponsored a nonbinding sense of the Congress vote in May 2003 stating that any agreement with Mexico over migration rights should include an agreement to open the state oil company PEMEX to U.S. investment. As expected, the Mexican government's response was a resounding "no," but the message from the U.S. Congress had been sent: if Mexico expects to resume serious migration talks in the future, it must be ready to offer something in exchange.

It is likely that benign neglect will characterize the Bush administration's attitude toward Mexico and the rest of Latin America for years to come. The U.S. government is largely focused on the reconstruction of Iraq, on peace talks between Israel and Palestine, and on the nuclear standoff on the Korean peninsula. Other issues will receive less attention.

Beyond the photo-ops, meetings between Presidents Fox and Bush have not produced the expected changes in bilateral relations. What the first half of President Fox's experiment with the United States teaches

is that goodwill is not the most important factor shaping bilateral relations. Democratization did have an impact on the warm reception Fox's
ideas received in Washington. But when it comes to specific deals, electoral and political interests in the United States carry greater weight
than democracy in Mexico.

Postscript

On January 7, 2004, President George W. Bush proposed a new temporary worker program. This proposal lacks the integral approach advocated
by the original Mexican initiative. It may help President Bush attract
more Latino votes, but it does not address the core issues that would
improve the current situation of millions of Mexican immigrants, or even
produce the long-awaited genuine change in the bilateral relationship.

Notes

The views expressed in this chapter are purely academic and unrelated to the
author's position at Mexico's Federal Electoral Institute.

1. Rafael Fernández de Castro argues that the institutionalization of the
bilateral relationship explains the dynamics of cooperation between Mexico and
the United States; see Rafael Fernández de Castro, "Perspectivas teóricas en los
estudios de la relación México-Estados Unidos: El caso de la cooperación inter-
gubernamental," in Instituto Matías Romero de Estudios Diplomáticos/Centro
de Estudios Internacionales (eds.), *La Política Exterior de México: Enfoques
para su análisis,* Mexico City: COLMEX, 1997.

2. See Blanca Heredia, "El dilema entre crecimiento y autonomía: Reforma
económica y reestructuración de la política exterior de México," in Instituto
Matías Romero de Estudios Diplomáticos/Centro de Estudios Internacionales
(eds.), *La Política Exterior de México: Enfoques para su análisis,* Mexico City:
COLMEX, 1997. Heredia argues that the debt crisis, which erupted in 1982,
made it clear that Mexico had to change its economic model, which, in turn,
implied a closer relationship with the United States. Fernández de Castro (see
Note 1) says that institutionalization and increased cooperation were best
reflected in trade but not in areas related to U.S. national security, such as
migration and the fight against drug trafficking.

3. Blanca Torres, "La participación de actores nuevos y tradicionales en las
relaciones internacionales de México," in Instituto Matías Romero de Estudios
Diplomáticos/Centro de Estudios Internacionales (eds.), *La Política Exterior de
México: Enfoques para su análisis,* Mexico City: COLMEX, 1997.

4. Fernández de Castro, "Perspectivas teóricas en los estudios."

5. This argument is made by Jorge Chabat in "La nueva agenda internacional y la política exterior mexicana," in Instituto Matías Romero de Estudios
Diplomáticos/Centro de Estudios Internacionales (eds.), *La Política Exterior de*

México: Enfoques para su análisis, Mexico: COLMEX, 1997. Heredia (see Note 2) notes that for much of the twentieth century—at least until the early 1980s—Mexico had an economic policy and a foreign policy that were mutually reinforcing. The former was based on state intervention and import substitution and generated growth without inflation for several decades (1954–1970). The latter was based on nationalism and self-determination and promoted a certain degree of state autonomy vis-à-vis the United States. However, the debt crisis erupted in 1982 and Mexico had to review its economic model. Gradually, new market reforms became increasingly incompatible with the traditional stance toward the United States.

6. Guadalupe González, "Foreign Politics Strategies in a Globalized World: The Case of Mexico," in Joseph Tulchin and Ralph H. Espach (eds.), *Latin America in the New International System,* Boulder, CO: Lynne Rienner Publishers, 2001.

7. For a description of how the Mexican Congress has become a relevant actor in Mexican politics, see Luis Carlos Ugalde, *The Mexican Congress: Old Player, New Power,* Washington, DC: Center for Strategic and International Studies, 2000.

8. It should also be noted that transnational crime organizations have arisen, generating a multibillion dollar business that includes drug trafficking, arms trafficking, and financial transactions.

9. See Ugalde, *The Mexican Congress.*

10. See Robert Putnam, "Diplomacy and Domestic Politics: The Logic of Two-Level Games," *International Organization* 42, no. 3 (summer 1988).

11. According to the Mexican Constitution, the president has powers to "conduct foreign policy and to negotiate international treaties with foreign countries submitting them to Senate ratification" (Constitutional Article 89). The Senate has powers to analyze the foreign policy determined by the president based on his or her reports and to approve international treaties and diplomatic conventions made by the president. It also has the power to ratify appointments of ambassadors and consuls (Constitutional Article 76).

12. During PRI administrations, Mexico abstained from expressing opposition to human rights abuses and political rights violations in Cuba. It was a silence consistent with the principle of nonintervention and with the aim of maintaining independence from Washington on certain political issues. The new Fox administration made a sweeping change in this policy, expressing its dissatisfaction with human rights violations in Cuba and supporting a condemnation of that country based on the Geneva Convention in 2001.

13. Presidential nominees for the embassies in Cuba and Egypt faced criticisms and suffered delays, although both ambassadors were ratified after negotiations between Congress and the administration.

14. Consulta Mitofsky, "Sentimientos hacia Estados Unidos después de los atentados a Nueva York y del Bombardeo a Afganistán," national telephone polls, October 9, 2001, and April 8, 2003: www.consulta.com.mx.

15. National telephone poll conducted in April 2002 by GEA-ISA, a Mexican consulting and polling firm.

16. By using the European Union as his model, Fox looked misinformed about the economic conditions that had made such convergence possible and were absent in North America. To many analysts, the Mexican president-elect appeared naïve.

17. Today, the minimum wage in the United States is 10.5 times higher than Mexico's, but that difference has declined since 1996 when the disparity was 12.3 to 1. As of early 2003, the U.S. minimum wage was $41.20 per day, while in Mexico it was $3.92 (41.9 pesos converted at an exchange rate of 10.68 pesos to US$1). In 1996, the U.S. daily minimum wage was $38 and Mexico's was $3.09 (24.3 pesos converted at an exchange rate of 7.85 pesos to US$1).

18. To understand the success of the Fox administration during the Guanajuato meeting in making Bush commit to beginning talks on migration along the lines suggested by Mexico, it is helpful to keep in mind the controversial manner in which Bush took power and how it might have delayed the initial planning of his administration, including his foreign policy strategy toward Mexico. When Bush first visited Mexico, he had been in power for less than a month and it is unlikely that a clear strategy existed yet on how to deal with Mexico. The lack of expertise and planning may partially explain President Bush's rapid acceptance of the terms suggested by Fox. In contrast, the Mexican delegation had clear ideas regarding the content of the proposed accord.

19. Data and comments provided by Carlos González, head of the Latino office at Mexico's Embassy to the United States, January 2003.

20. U.S. Census Bureau, Press Release, January 21, 2003: www.census.gov/Press-Release/www/2003/cb03-16.html.

21. B. Lindsay Lowell and Robert Suro, "How Many Undocumented: The Numbers Behind the U.S.-Mexico Migration Talks," The Pew Hispanic Center, March 21, 2002, pp. 5–6.

22. Ibid., pp. 3–4.

23. Such strategy has been subsequently criticized in private by Luis Ernesto Derbez, Castañeda's successor as foreign secretary, who believes that the maximalist approach makes the deal unviable. Piecemeal advancements in migration are more realistic in this view.

24. Vicente Fox, *New York Times,* September 4, 2001.

25. *Washington Post,* September 4, 2001.

26. Editorial, *New York Times,* September 7, 2001.

27. Speech before the U.S. Congress, September 6, 2003: www.presidencia.gob.mx.

28. During the months following September 11, the Mexican government attempted to resume talks on several occasions. Many voices claimed the time was even more propitious for migration talks if Mexico could sell the idea of a North American security region in which Mexico would shield its southern borders to block any terrorist from entering the United States via Mexico. Secretary Castañeda "tried repeatedly to convince the Bush administration that a new arrangement on immigration, including legal status and documentation for millions of Mexicans in the United States, would enhance American national security." *New York Times,* January 9, 2003.

29. Diplomatic sources confirm that during his private encounter with President Fox in Los Cabos, President Bush demanded the resignation of Adolfo Aguilar Zinser, Mexico's ambassador to the United Nations, who had been an outspoken opponent of the U.S. position on Iraq and a supporter of the French and Russian approach. President Fox refused this request, saying the Mexican ambassador had acted on his behalf.

30. The Binational Commission is a cabinet-level group formed in 1981 that meets annually either in the United States or in Mexico. It is different from the migration working group formed in 2001 to make specific recommendations on that topic.

31. *Financial Times Information,* November 8, 2002.

32. Nevertheless, the president's party, the PAN, suffered a setback in the 2003 midterm elections, as it lost more than fifty seats in the Chamber of Deputies. This loss came amidst a high approval rating for President Fox of about 65 percent in June 2003. If Fox's popularity had suffered as a result of supporting the war on Iraq, his party might have lost even more votes.

33. See Fox, *New York Times,* September 4, 2001. For Davidow's farewell remarks, see *Milenio,* November 16, 2002.

34. Robert S. Leiken, "End of an Affair? Immigration, Security and the U.S.-Mexican Relationship," *The National Interest* (winter 2002–2003): 87–97.

35. Ibid.

6

The Changing Bilateral Relationship: A U.S. View

Susan Kaufman Purcell

Every twelve years, presidential elections in Mexico and the United States coincide. The last time this occurred was in 2000, when Vicente Fox and George W. Bush became the presidents of Mexico and the United States respectively. The election of 2000, however, was also special because it marked the end of more than seventy years of control of Mexico's presidency by a single party, the Institutional Revolutionary Party (PRI). Mexico's political transformation into a competitive democratic political system affected not only its domestic politics and policies, but also had a big, and initially very favorable, impact on the country's foreign policy and particularly on its relationship with the United States.

Less than one year after both elections, another momentous event occurred, this time in the United States. The terrorist attacks of September 11, 2001, abruptly altered U.S. foreign policy priorities. Overnight, security concerns rose to the top of Washington's agenda, and the Bush administration's attention veered from its newly democratic southern neighbor to the undemocratic and problematic Middle East. The war against Iraq, launched in March 2003 in alliance with Great Britain and other coalition partners, reinforced the shift in Washington's focus.

Whether this change in priorities is a long-term or short-term development remains to be seen. On the one hand, the great and continually growing interdependence between Mexico and the United States makes it unlikely that action on the bilateral issues initially addressed by the two presidents can be postponed indefinitely. On the other hand, Mexico's active role as a member of the UN Security Council in opposing U.S. military action in Iraq makes it unlikely that President Bush will be as personally engaged in the bilateral relationship as he was initially.

The most likely scenario, therefore, is that bilateral issues will soon recapture the attention of the Bush administration, although not of the

president himself. In addition, Washington's interest in resolving difficult bilateral issues will be greatest when they can be convincingly por-
trayed as relevant to general U.S. security concerns.

Bilateral Relations Before 2000

Washington's current focus on security is not unfamiliar to Mexico.
During the Cold War, U.S. policy toward Latin America was dominated
by a preoccupation with the potential spread of communism and, specifically, of Soviet and Cuban influence in Latin America. In order to
"contain" communism, Washington often supported right-wing military
regimes friendly to the United States over left-wing elected governments that were viewed as sympathetic to Moscow and Havana. The
United States also worked with Latin American military establishments
to defeat a number of Marxist guerrilla movements in the region. At the
same time, increases in U.S. economic aid to Latin America sought to
ameliorate the poverty that provided fertile soil for the guerrilla movements to take root. The Alliance for Progress of the 1960s was perhaps
the quintessential example of Washington's Cold War approach to the
region, with its combination of short-term military aid and long-term
economic assistance.

Mexico, like the majority of Latin American countries, welcomed
the emphasis on fighting poverty, but criticized U.S. military involvement in the region. Like most of Latin America, it viewed the Cuban
Revolution as an essentially nationalistic event. Mexico dismissed, at
least publicly, the idea of a Cuban or Soviet threat to the hemisphere,
although internally its PRI-dominated government worked hard to
destroy its own Marxist guerrilla movements during the 1960s. In the
1970s, however, with the election of Luis Echeverría as president, Mexico's foreign policy became more active and supportive of so-called
third-world positions that were often anti-U.S. and, from Washington's
perspective, overly tolerant of Soviet expansionism, particularly in
developing countries. Echeverría's hostility toward multinational corporations, his embrace of an increasingly statist economic development
strategy, and his pursuit of closer relations with Cuba further strained
U.S.-Mexican relations.

Echeverría's strategy, which was continued by his successor, José
López Portillo, ended with the debt crisis of 1982. By that time Mexico
had become an important oil producer, thereby increasing its strategic
importance to the United States. López Portillo's successor, Miguel de la
Madrid, was obliged by the debt crisis to play a less active role in foreign affairs. This served to downplay somewhat the growing differences

between Mexico and the United States over the civil conflict in Central America, where Washington sought a military solution and Mexico worked for a negotiated settlement. At the same time, Mexico's need for foreign capital in the aftermath of the debt crisis caused de la Madrid to begin opening Mexico's economy to foreign investment, reduce the state's role in the economy, and in particular, seek improved relations with the United States. These changes in Mexico's foreign policy and development strategy ultimately marked the beginning of a more cooperative and mature relationship between the two neighboring countries.

This new relationship was consolidated during the presidencies of Carlos Salinas de Gortari and the first President Bush. The end of the Cold War helped. With the collapse of the Soviet Union, the United States was able to deemphasize security concerns and instead turn its attention to trade and development issues. Salinas, who grasped the implications of the Soviet collapse for Mexico, tried initially to intensify economic relations with Europe but came to understand Europe's preoccupation with itself and quickly shifted gears, requesting a free-trade agreement with the United States. As the NAFTA negotiations progressed, Mexico's foreign policy underwent significant changes. Salinas rejected the anti-Americanism and third-world orientation of some of his predecessors, joined the Organization for Economic Cooperation and Development, and downplayed differences with Washington over third-party countries, particularly Cuba.

This trend toward improved bilateral relations continued throughout the 1990s. On the U.S. side, President Clinton provided badly needed economic support to Mexico in the aftermath of the 1994 peso devaluation and near-default on its debt. The Clinton administration also responded positively to growing demands for democracy in Mexico by broadening its contacts with opposition political parties while maintaining its relations with the PRI. On the Mexican side, President Ernesto Zedillo legitimized the opposition's winning control of Congress in the 1997 elections and took important steps, supported and encouraged by Washington, toward ensuring that Mexican elections were free and fair. With the election of Vicente Fox and George W. Bush in late 2000, the stage was set for a big step forward in the bilateral relationship.

The Impact of Mexican Democracy on U.S.-Mexican Relations

The election of Vicente Fox as Mexico's first postrevolutionary president from an opposition party was followed shortly thereafter by the election of George W. Bush as president of the United States. Many observers quickly noted that the two men were ideally suited to work together for improved bilateral relations. Neither president was an inhabitant of his nation's capital city. Both had served as governors prior to their elevation to the presidency. Both were ranchers and had prior experience in the private sector (in fact, Fox had worked for Coca-Cola, long an icon of U.S. capitalism). Both men were religious, although Fox was a practicing Catholic while Bush was a born-again Christian. Neither was an intellectual, in contrast to their respective predecessors. And both had a folksy style that allowed them to appeal to a broad spectrum of their respective country's population.

President Fox had lived for a number of years in the United States and spoke excellent English. He understood the United States and felt comfortable with its people and its culture. President Bush had been the governor of Texas, which borders on Mexico and has a large Mexican-American population. He spoke some Spanish, felt comfortable with his Mexican-American constituents, and had managed to win a large percentage of the Hispanic vote, during both his gubernatorial and presidential races. This in itself was an unusual accomplishment for a Republican candidate, particularly a conservative one. Although considerably less traveled than President Fox, Bush had visited Mexico several times, making it the foreign country he knew best. He understood the significance of Fox's election and recognized that a newly democratic Mexico opened the door to new opportunities in the bilateral relationship.

Bush was correct about what a democratic Mexico means for the United States. Specifically, he understood that U.S. citizens often distrust and dislike undemocratic governments. They also dislike governments that appear to be anti-U.S. In the 1970s, Mexico fit both categories. In the 1980s, the anti-Americanism of the 1970s was replaced by a visible effort on the part of Mexico to improve relations with the United States. Mexico's transition to democracy in 2000 put the missing piece into place and gave President Bush the opportunity to fashion a special relationship with Mexico with unprecedented support from the U.S. electorate. Such support, in turn, would make it easier for Congress to support at least some of the president's new bilateral agenda.

While democracy in Mexico gave President Bush more latitude in the United States to pursue a special relationship with Mexico, democracy in Mexico presented a more mixed blessing for President Fox. On the one hand, the transition from one-party rule to competitive democracy provided an opportunity for the new president to reformulate Mexico's foreign policy priorities, both in general and particularly regarding the United States. On the other hand, Mexico's more pluralistic democracy made it more difficult for President Fox to obtain congressional approval for his initiatives. Since the 1997 congressional elections, no single party has held a majority of the seats in the Chamber of Deputies, while in the Senate the PRI has remained the dominant party. Furthermore, with democracy came a weakening of presidential control over Congress, a development that was compounded by earlier economic reforms that had reduced the economic power of the state vis-à-vis private economic groups.

Despite the potential for congressional obstructionism, President Fox lost no time in launching his new foreign policy approach. The appointment of Jorge Castañeda as foreign secretary reinforced early indications that a democratic Mexico would play a more active role on the world stage. Castañeda was a well-known academic, writer, and political activist, as well as the son of a former foreign secretary. He immediately announced Mexico's intention to campaign for a seat on the UN Security Council. During the years of PRI dominance, Mexico had been reluctant to "interfere" in the affairs of other countries, in the belief that doing so would encourage other countries, particularly the United States, to criticize Mexico's own political system and human rights record. Given the conduct and results of the 2000 presidential election, however, the Fox administration no longer considered itself vulnerable to such criticism or pressure.

The emphasis of Mexico's more active foreign policy also reflected the country's democratic transition. Support for democracy and human rights became important aspects of the foreign policy agenda. Within Latin America, the clearest manifestation of this new emphasis involved Mexico's Cuba policy. In fact, Mexico's policy toward the Castro government had begun to change under President Zedillo, whose efforts to democratize Mexico had led him to instruct his foreign minister to begin speaking with Cuban dissidents. The Fox administration took the new policy further by voting in favor of a UN resolution criticizing Cuba's human rights behavior. In the past, Mexico had at most abstained during similar votes.

Mexico's reformed Cuba policy angered the Cuban government but was enthusiastically welcomed by Washington. If the Bush administration concluded that Los Pinos, the presidential residence, and the White House were now in agreement over Cuba, however, it was mistaken. Mexico managed to maintain its independent stance toward the Castro regime by joining its criticism of human rights abuses on the island with criticism of the U.S. embargo. From Washington's vantage point, however, the new Mexican approach toward Castro's Cuba was a big improvement over the traditional stance.

Mexico's more active support for democracy, although welcomed by Washington, initially put the United States and Mexico on different sides of the Venezuelan coup issue. The Bush administration had at first welcomed the overthrow of President Hugo Chávez by a broad-based coalition of opponents of the regime, which included parts of the Venezuelan military. Although Washington had repeatedly discouraged a military coup, it believed that those who ousted the increasingly autocratic and hostile Chávez were committed to reestablishing a democratic government, a belief that quickly proved to be erroneous. Mexico, however, joined with other members of the so-called Rio Group in condemning the Chávez overthrow and refusing to grant recognition to his successor as president. Without such support, the opposition-led government collapsed and Chávez returned to power. The United States ultimately condemned the opposition's resort to unconstitutional behavior, but its condemnation was regarded as "too little, too late."

Despite their differences in the implementation of their human rights and prodemocracy policies, however, Mexico's new activism in favor of both was generally welcomed and appreciated by Washington. Both issues constituted important elements of U.S. policy toward the hemisphere, although their implementation sometimes fell short of perfection. From the U.S. perspective, it was better to have a democratic Mexico fighting actively for democratic principles than an authoritarian Mexico that sheltered dictators hostile to U.S. interests behind a foreign policy based on the principle of nonintervention.

Mexico's new activism on the world stage also manifested itself in the area of hemispheric security. In what ultimately came to be considered an unfortunate example of very bad timing, Foreign Secretary Castañeda announced just days before the September 11 attacks that Mexico was planning to withdraw from the 1947 Rio Treaty, which it regarded as an obsolete relic of the now-defunct Cold War. The attacks on the World Trade Center caused Mexico to delay its withdrawal from the treaty. Mexico finally withdrew from the treaty one year after it had initially announced its intention to do so, only days before the first anniversary of the terrorist attacks—a second example of bad timing that may have reflected the Fox administration's failure to appreciate the impact the terrorist attacks had had on the Bush administration's world view. Mexico used the occasion to call for the elaboration of a multidimensional approach to hemispheric security in place of the Rio Treaty, one that would be more relevant to current and future threats. Mexico's new approach broadened the definition of hemispheric security threats to include poverty, terrorism and drug trafficking, deficiencies in public health, environmental degradation, natural disasters, and economic crises. These issues were discussed at the Organization of American States special conference on hemispheric security in 2003.

The Bush administration was not pleased by Mexico's initial announcement of its intention to withdraw from the Rio Treaty, and was even less pleased when Mexico withdrew, given the events of the preceding September 11. The treaty, a U.S. creation that had established the principle of collective security in the hemisphere, had served Washington well since its creation. In the aftermath of the terrorist attacks, the Bush administration had been planning to use the treaty as the foundation for a stronger, cooperative antiterrorist policy in Latin America. Furthermore, Washington did not like Mexico's redefinition of the concept of security, which it felt broadened the word to the point where it meant everything and nothing.

The conventional wisdom is that Mexico was sending several messages to Washington and the world. First, despite the growing convergence in values, the United States cannot and should not take Mexico for granted. Second, despite its growing interdependence with the United States and the great asymmetry in the bilateral relationship, Mexico remains an independent country with its own foreign policy. Third, active involvement in global issues is a necessary counterweight to Mexico's bilateral relationship with its northern neighbor.

A more active foreign policy, with a new emphasis on democracy and human rights and an expanded definition of hemispheric threats, was only one component of Mexico's post-2000 foreign policy. The other major component was an effort to redefine and deepen NAFTA along lines that paralleled the experience of the European Union. This involved closer cooperation in dealing with drugs, energy, and especially immigration and economic development.

Mexico's new North American agenda was unveiled by President Fox in 2000 during the Summit of the Americas in Ottawa. Fox spoke of an integrated North American region loosely modeled on the integration experience of the European Union. His ultimate objectives included improved policy coordination, a common monetary policy, a common external tariff, mobile pools of labor, and fiscal transfers from the industrialized North (i.e., the United States and Canada) to the developing South (i.e., Mexico).[1]

During subsequent meetings between Presidents Fox and Bush, as well as other high-ranking officials of both governments, Mexico reiterated these goals. On September 4, 2001, during his first official presidential visit to Washington, for example, Fox called for an immigration agreement before the end of the year, a shortening of a longer deadline that took President Bush completely by surprise. Foreign Secretary Castañeda memorably summarized Mexico's position on North American integration as one that sought "the whole enchilada," a colloquial way of saying that Mexico wanted a comprehensive agreement of which immigration would constitute only one element.

Mexico's more ambitious and aggressive policy stance regarding North American integration would have been unthinkable in the absence of its transition to democracy. Mexican officials knew that the free flow of labor was a politically explosive issue in the United States. This had been made very clear to them during the NAFTA negotiations in the early 1990s. However, Fox and his advisers also understood that Fox's election had begun to change Mexico's image abroad and had created a great deal of goodwill toward the country in the United States. The decision to go for "the whole enchilada" was an attempt to capitalize on this goodwill and move Mexico's relationship with the United States to a new level.

The more ambitious agenda also represented an attempt by the Mexican government to use foreign policy to help solve some serious domestic problems. Since the 1970s, the Mexican economy has not been able to generate sufficient jobs for all Mexicans seeking employment. Immigration to the United States, whether legal or illegal, provided Mexico with two important benefits. First, it acted as a safety valve, allowing Mexicans unhappy with their situation to leave the country. Second, it provided an important source of income to Mexico in the form of cash remittances that Mexicans living and working in the United States regularly send to their relatives back home. The amount of such remittances reached an estimated $14.5 billion in 2003. Their growing importance to Mexico is evidenced by the fact that in the first half of 2003 the total amount of remittances entering Mexico exceeded for the first time the total amount of foreign direct investment entering the country.

The Bush administration welcomed closer cooperation with Mexico within the context of a deeper NAFTA. U.S. officials made clear, however, that it was politically unhelpful for Mexico to raise the issue of the free flow of labor during a period when the U.S. economy was in recession and millions were unemployed. Mexico ultimately responded by shifting its focus to immigration issues that were more politically feasible to implement. These included an increase in the number of visas granted for Mexican workers, as well as the question of how to "regularize" the position of the estimated 3–4 million undocumented Mexicans living in the United States. Discussion centered on the possibility and desirability of a new amnesty for those Mexicans who had lived continuously in the United States for a number of years. Other issues involved in regularizing the status of undocumented Mexicans include

allowing them to obtain driver's licenses and open bank accounts, as w
as attend U.S. public schools. While the amnesty issue will require a decision at the national level, the other issues have begun to be addressed by
local governments in the absence of a presidential or congressional decision laying out a national policy. Specifically, more than a hundred U.S.
cities have begun to accept identity cards, or *matrículas consulares,*
issued by Mexican consular offices as valid IDs for opening bank
accounts, obtaining driver's licenses, and receiving some city services.[2]

At the same time that the Fox administration was asking for a more
liberal U.S. immigration policy with respect to Mexico, it also made an
unprecedented effort on the Mexican side of the border to staunch the
flow of illegal migrants into the United States. Washington had long
been frustrated by Mexico's unwillingness to take any action to reduce
illegal migration from Mexico. Mexico's traditional stance on the issue
was that its citizens were free to travel to whatever countries they
wished. With the election of Vicente Fox, however, Mexico changed its
position. In a joint communiqué dated June 22, 2001, for example, it
joined with the United States in agreeing to increase public safety campaigns to inform potential migrants of the dangers and risks of crossing
the border.[3] In addition, one border state, Baja California Norte, has
designated certain particularly dangerous sections of its border with
California as off-limits areas (*zonas de exclusión*). Agents stationed in
these areas prohibit trucks and buses from dropping off potential
migrants at isolated areas and intercept others trying to cross the desert.

Mexico explained its change of policy by reference to its new concern for human rights. Specifically, the government justified interfering
with Mexicans' right to travel because of concerns over the number of
Mexicans who were injured or died while trying to cross the harsh
deserts that covered much of the border region. The unstated reason for
the new policy undoubtedly was Mexico's desire to exhibit a more
cooperative attitude toward the United States in order to encourage
Washington to look more favorably on the ambitious immigration reform being sought from the Bush administration.

Immigration proposals involving open borders were not the only
suggestions about how NAFTA might be deepened that the Bush administration regarded as politically unfeasible. It also disagreed with Mexico's proposal concerning the transfer of resources on the model of the
European Union. Specifically, Mexico would like to see the United
States and Canada transfer substantial resources to Mexico to be used to
develop infrastructure and generally help offset the disadvantages that
Mexico faces in trying to compete with the more economically developed countries to its north. In Europe, the so-called cohesion funds are

generally considered to have played an important role in helping Europe's poorer countries, such as Ireland, Spain, and Portugal, integrate successfully with the region's bigger and more developed economies. The Bush administration, however, knew that political support for a NAFTA-type cohesion fund was lacking. Instead it proposed a more politically palatable approach to development assistance that would include poor regions in the United States as well as in Mexico. Such development assistance could be administered by NAFTA institutions such as the North American Development Bank.

Mexico's transition to democracy also facilitated increased cooperation with the United States on the illegal drug issue. Some progress had been made during the presidency of Ernesto Zedillo. An elite counternarcotics force was established following scandals supporting U.S. claims that the police and army had been corrupted by the drug cartels. President Fox, however, was in a stronger position than his predecessor to attack drug trafficking in Mexico. As the first non-PRI president, he was expected to differentiate and distance himself and his administration from the intertwined and corrupt relationships that had characterized the PRI after more than seventy years of controlling the presidency of Mexico. In addition to increasing the arrests of drug traffickers, Mexico began cooperating with the United States on drug interdiction. Unlike the past, the main link was not the attorney general's office, but the Mexican army. This change reflected both the greater capability and efficiency of a reformed and better-trained army to deal with the drug traffickers and the chronic instability and weakness of the attorney general's office.

Energy cooperation surfaced as a relatively new item on the bilateral agenda. The United States had first raised the issue during the NAFTA negotiations, in part to offset Mexico's demands for a more liberal treatment of Mexican illegal migrants in the United States. In the early 1990s, energy cooperation was as difficult an issue for Mexico as open borders was for the United States. Finally, both countries agreed to exclude both issues from the NAFTA negotiations. By the time Fox was elected president, however, a number of things had changed. Mexico needed more investment in its state-owned oil and electric-power industries in order to avoid important energy shortages in the near future. Instability in the Middle East caused the United States to seek sources of energy closer to home. And Vicente Fox, a man who had worked in the private sector and who did not belong to the political party that had nationalized the oil industry, was more favorably disposed to the entry of at least some foreign capital into the energy sector. In fact, during his presidential campaign, he had publicly advocated the privatization of

PEMEX, retreating on that issue only because of the political uproar it produced in Mexico.

Despite Fox's change of position during the campaign, Mexico's more open political system did facilitate the airing and discussion of the issues of what to do about impending energy shortages and the need for massive new investment in the energy sector. It was harder to protect sacred cows when there had been a changing of the guard. The issue of energy cooperation had also been depoliticized somewhat by removing it from a strictly bilateral context and airing it instead in the trilateral context of NAFTA. In the aftermath of the Iraq war, however, as Mexico resumed its efforts to obtain an immigration agreement with the United States, a number of U.S. congressmen introduced legislation proposing to link such an agreement to bilateral energy cooperation, politicizing the issue once again. It clearly will take some time before concrete decisions are taken in the area of U.S.-Mexican energy cooperation.

While Mexico's democratic transition has facilitated increased bilateral discussions on a number of issues and enabled Mexico to present more ambitious programs for such cooperation, there are also a number of ways in which a democratic Mexico has made U.S.-Mexican relations more complicated and difficult to manage. Most involve the increased importance and power of the Mexican Congress in the foreign policy–making process. Until 1997, PRI presidents had used their control of Congress to initiate legislation, which was then approved by overwhelming majorities. In the 1997 congressional elections, however, the PRI lost its majority in the Chamber of Deputies, although it continued to hold the largest bloc of seats. In 2000, when Vicente Fox was elected on the PAN ticket, he faced a Congress in which no party had a majority but in which PRI influence remained strong. The congressional elections of July 2003 made a difficult situation worse. Fox's party lost a significant number of seats in the Chamber, while the number of left-of-center PRD congressmen increased substantially. Despite losing a few seats, the PRI remained the largest minority bloc in the Chamber. Since 2000, therefore, Fox has had to govern with a divided Congress, one in which the opposition parties have been able to defeat presidential legislative initiatives if they have chosen to unite for that purpose.

In the area of foreign policy, the Mexican Congress on several occasions has used its newly independent status to sanction President Fox for decisions it did not like. One such case involved a trip that President Fox was scheduled to make to the United States early in 2002. Angry at the president for having catered to U.S. needs and for Mexico's new hard line toward Cuba on the issue of human rights, Congress denied the president permission to travel to the United States.[4] Several months later, in August 2002, the president was obliged to cancel a trip to Texas to protest the execution of a Mexican citizen by the State of Texas. Fox had wanted to make the trip, but was obliged by public opinion and congressional opposition to refrain from doing so. Congress's behavior also reflected its general unhappiness with Fox's failure to work closely with the legislative branch.

President Fox summed up his situation like this: "In Mexico, I find contradictory reactions in regard to relations with the United States. On one side, citizens have great respect for the United States; they have a great feeling of friendship. In the opposition and the political arena I often find criticism of the closeness of relations with the United States. That is a reality. It is a reality that flares up every time a new issue arises. And the issue comes up every day."[5]

Potentially more serious has been growing resistance to the NAFTA-mandated opening of various sectors of Mexican agriculture to competition from the United States. Having done little over the decade since NAFTA was signed to prepare for the reduction or elimination of several agricultural tariffs on January 1, 2003, the Mexican government was nevertheless surprised when Mexican farmers and several anti-NAFTA groups took to the streets in protest and demanded the renegotiation of the agreement. The PRD and other representatives of opposition parties supported their demands. The fact that the Bush administration had recently increased government subsidies to U.S. agricultural producers added fuel to the fire. The issue was defused, at least temporarily, when the Fox administration entered into negotiations with the Bush administration and hammered out a number of compromises. The issue of NAFTA's agricultural provisions will surface again, however, since tariffs on corn, Mexico's main agricultural staple, are set to be lifted in January 2008. And unlike the situation that existed when the administration of Carlos Salinas de Gortari first negotiated NAFTA, congressional opponents of NAFTA now have the power to act on their demands. This does not mean that NAFTA's survival is at stake, but it does mean that the resolution of bilateral conflicts concerning NAFTA will be more complicated and difficult in the coming years.[6]

The absence of a presidential majority in Congress and ambivalent attitudes toward the United States are not the only realities complicating U.S. relations with a newly democratic Mexico. Also important is the lack of accountability of Mexican legislators to the voters. Mexico's constitution forbids the consecutive reelection of members of the Chamber of Deputies. In order for congressmen to serve more than one term, they must sit out a term and then stand for reelection. This means that whether a congressman behaves well or badly in terms of what the voters want is essentially irrelevant to his political future. Voters cannot remove unresponsive congressmen from office, nor can they reward well-performing ones by reelecting them. The situation encourages irresponsible behavior on the part of legislators, who are free to pursue their own interests rather than those of the citizens who elected them. This makes it difficult for the Mexican president to work with them on foreign policy issues, as well as on domestic matters with foreign policy implications.

In addition, the fact that congressmen cannot serve consecutive terms means that needed expertise on foreign policy issues cannot be developed. This contrasts greatly with the situation of U.S. congressmen, many of whom have acquired considerable knowledge of foreign policy over the years. The problem in Mexico is compounded by a lack of sufficient staff to aid Congress in its work. The U.S. Congress has a staff of thousands, as well as a research arm that is part of the Library of Congress. Its Mexican counterpart, in contrast, must deal with a growing agenda and very few human and other resources to help it legislate. This is undoubtedly a legacy of the PRI years, when Congress rubber-stamped presidential initiatives and was not permitted to play an independent role in any kind of decisionmaking, including foreign policy.

It is in the interest of both Mexico and the United States that this situation be remedied sooner rather than later. Given the growing importance of both Mexico's foreign policy agenda and its bilateral relationship with the United States, Mexico can no longer afford to have a legislative branch that lacks accountability, experience, and adequate staffing. The current situation reinforces a sense in the United States that Mexico is not an equal, mature, and trustworthy partner on foreign policy issues. This is unfortunate and harmful to the U.S.-Mexican relationship, given the high degree of cooperation that is, and will continue to be, necessary between the two countries.

The impact of Mexico's democratic transition on U.S.-Mexican relations has therefore cut two ways. On the one hand, it has created new opportunities for a more ambitious, cooperative bilateral relationship based on greater equality and mutual respect. At the same time, however, it has complicated the bilateral relationship by making Mexico's foreign policy decisionmaking process considerably more complex than it had been under the so-called peace of the PRI. Whereas in the past Washington did not have to factor into its decisions the potential impact of the Mexican Congress and, to a lesser extent, of Mexican public opinion, today both must be taken into account by U.S. policymakers. There is little doubt, however, that Washington much prefers to have a democratic Mexico as a neighbor, despite the increased complexity of the bilateral relationship. Democratic neighbors might disagree, but there is a basic compatibility and commonality of interests and values between them, as well as greater potential for long-term cooperation and mutual understanding.

The Impact of September 11 on U.S.-Mexican Relations

If Mexico's democratic transition served to emphasize the similarities between Mexico and the United States, the terrorist attacks of September 11, 2001, emphasized their remaining differences. Security concerns moved to the top of Washington's foreign policy agenda and the global fight against terrorism became the number-one priority. As a result, the Bush administration's attention was diverted from Mexico and the rest of Latin America toward the Middle East and other regions where radical Islam was a potential or actual threat. The terrorist attacks, however, did not have a similar effect on Mexico, whose top foreign policy concern remained its relationship with the United States.

The post–September 11 situation was reminiscent of the Cold War, when security issues—specifically a preoccupation with the spread of communism—also topped Washington's foreign policy agenda. Then, as now, Mexico and the rest of Latin America did not share the U.S. concern and wanted Washington to focus instead on development issues. When the United States did not do so, Latin America accused Washington of neglecting the hemisphere—a charge that has surfaced once again in the aftermath of September 11.

Whether or not the United States has indeed neglected Latin America since the terrorist attacks is debatable, given the Bush administration's recent successful campaign to obtain Trade Promotion Authority, which made possible a U.S.-Chile free trade agreement and which is a necessary prerequisite to creating a Free Trade Area of the Americas. In the case of Mexico, however, the charge of U.S. neglect is more valid. Before September 11, Mexican foreign minister Jorge Castañeda was meeting regularly with Colin Powell, his U.S. counterpart. After September 11, the one-on-one meetings stopped. This was understandable given Secretary Powell's important role in leading the U.S. war against terrorism. Nevertheless, it was a severe disappointment for both Castañeda and the Mexican government. Castañeda subsequently attributed his January 2003 resignation to his frustration in trying to work with a Bush administration whose attention had turned elsewhere. It is important to note that the regular bilateral meetings between the Mexican foreign minister and U.S. secretary of state were somewhat unusual in the first place. Past foreign ministers of Mexico had generally met with the assistant secretary of state for Latin American affairs instead of with their nominal U.S. counterpart. The Powell-Castañeda meetings occurred partly because President Bush's nominee for the position of assistant secretary, Otto Reich, had not been approved by Congress. But the Powell-Castañeda meetings were also the result of a decision by the U.S. president to elevate the importance of the U.S.-Mexico relationship.

The cornerstone of Castañeda's more ambitious U.S.-Mexico agenda prior to September 11 had been immigration policy. His short-term wish list had included an amnesty program for undocumented Mexicans living in the United States. Over the longer term, he envisioned the free flow of labor between the United States and Mexico. Unfortunately for Mexico, immigration reform was the area most affected by the terrorist attacks. The percentage of U.S. citizens wanting fewer immigrants in the United States rose from 41 percent in June 2001 to 58 percent by October 2001.[7] This was understandable, in view of the fact that the terrorists who carried out the September 11 attacks had been living both legally and illegally in the United States. The attacks also negatively affected many U.S. industries, thereby increasing the number of unemployed. This further eroded support for increased immigration.

The problem was also compounded by what was initially perceived as Mexico's ambivalent support for the United States immediately after the events of September 11. The contrast between the behavior of the Canadian prime minister and the Mexican president was striking. While the former immediately expressed support for and solidarity with the United States, and made a point of quickly visiting Washington, the Mexican president said nothing and stayed away. Canadian citizens were also extremely supportive of their neighbors, while U.S. newspapers were filled with stories about anti-U.S. comments on the part of the Mexican public and expressions of support for, or justification of the behavior of, the terrorists.

In the context of President Bush's declaration after the attacks that countries were either "with us or against us," Mexico's behavior was not regarded as that of a real friend. Fortunately, the Mexican government soon realized that its conspicuous absence following September 11 risked seriously undermining its long-term relationship with the United States and reversed course. President Fox visited both Washington and "Ground Zero." He expressed sympathy for those who had died there, including many Mexicans, and declared "the terrorist attacks of September 11 were an attack on humanity and therefore an attack on the national interests, peace, and aspirations of all Mexicans."[8]

Mexico also realized that additional cooperation was necessary if the bilateral relationship was to be put back on course. Adolfo Aguilar Zinser, Mexico's national security coordinator, reframed Mexico's bilateral agenda, placing security cooperation at the top of the agenda. Although none of the September 11 terrorists had entered the United States from Mexico, the Fox administration began tightening security on its northern border and began speaking of Mexico as part of a North American security area. Mexico also held hundreds of individuals of Middle Eastern origin in a U.S.-directed manhunt.[9] In addition, the Fox administration suggested that immigration and customs agents in the three NAFTA countries pass each other information on the movements of potential terrorists,[10] although it is not clear that much progress has been made to date on this front.

Intelligence sharing has increased since September 11 between the U.S. government and the Mexican army regarding drug trafficking. That, combined with greater control of the U.S.-Mexico border by the U.S. government, has produced a noticeable decline in the amount of illegal drugs entering the United States since the attacks. The increased control on the U.S. side of the border, however, has negatively affected trade between the United States and Mexico, as trucks carrying goods from Mexico initially had to suffer massive delays and still encounter some difficulties in trying to enter the United States. The solution involves moving toward a "smart border," with pre-clearance for goods, fast lanes for frequent travelers, and modern detection devices to improve screening and identification of people and goods entering the United States from Mexico.[11]

Progress toward such changes on the U.S.-Mexican border may be slow, however, mainly because "official corruption, alien smugglers, drug trafficking, organized crime and terrorist groups combine to make the Mexican border 'a diffuse and insidious threat,' as the State Department's coordinator for counter-terrorism told a congressional committee in October 2001."[12] Or, as one U.S. official put it, the United States cannot entrust its security "to foreign border officials who, for $50, will look the other way while some dubious character comes in."[13] Despite these problems, some form of pre-clearance for goods, high-tech identification cards, and other innovations that reduce the risk of the entry of potentially dangerous individuals into the United States ultimately will be adopted for the U.S.-Mexican border.

Although the southern border to date has not been used as an entry point by terrorists, U.S. officials fear that Al Qaeda operatives will eventually try to enter the United States by this route. It would not be a new idea. In World War I, Germany offered to return territory to Mexico that the United States had conquered if Mexico would attack and thereby tie down the United States. The Bush administration is already worried, with some justification, that the so-called Abdullah ring, which specializes in smuggling people from the Middle East across the U.S.-Mexican border, has ties with terrorist organizations. Because of these smugglers, the number of Middle Easterners who have crossed Mexico's borders illegally has soared.[14]

Although the problems in achieving a more secure U.S.-Mexican border have stalled Mexico's immigration agenda, the issue has recently resurfaced in the guise of a security issue. Specifically, Mexican government officials argue that the legalization of the large numbers of undocumented immigrants in the United States would give Washington a better sense of who is in the country and thereby enhance U.S. national security. Their argument has been well-received by a number of Republican and Democratic U.S. legislators who, like their Mexican counterparts, see domestic economic and political benefits from the legalization of undocumented immigrants, a majority of whom are Mexican, living in the United States. Both parties believe that legalization could help them win increased political support from Hispanics, the largest and fastest-growing minority group in the United States. Big business, generally supporters of the Republican Party, sees legalization as a source of needed unskilled labor. Democrats, for their part, believe that legalization would help swell the ranks of organized labor, traditionally a key constituency of the Democratic Party and in recent years experiencing a serious decline in membership.

Despite the resurfacing of the immigration reform issue, however, there is still no consensus regarding the criteria, if any, for granting legal status to the several million undocumented Mexican and other immigrants in the United States. One proposal involves a system of "earned regularization" over a period of three to five years. A point system would be established whereby undocumented migrants could earn points for learning English, holding a job and other behavior that helps integrate them into life in the United States. The points would be applied toward obtaining a permanent visa and eventually, U.S. citizenship. Another idea, reflected in President Bush's migration proposal of January 2004, would involve the creation of some kind of temporary worker program for Mexicans wishing to work in the United States.

It may not be enough, however, for Mexico to link immigration reform to security concerns in order to encourage the United States to implement the reforms it desires. It may also be necessary to tie immigration reform—a politically difficult issue for the United States—to energy reform, a similarly difficult issue for Mexico. Such a quid pro quo was first raised during the NAFTA negotiations a decade ago. It went nowhere because the U.S. electorate was unprepared to accept broad immigration reform and the Mexican people would not consider cooperating with the United States in the energy area. This situation has not changed significantly; however, in the not-too-distant future some kind of energy cooperation with Mexico may prove to be more feasible, particularly if it is placed in a trilateral (i.e., NAFTA) context instead of in a bilateral (i.e., U.S.-Mexican) context. Already, ministers of all three countries have met to discuss possible areas for future cooperation. In addition, a North American working group on energy has been created to work out a regional approach to energy issues.[15]

The main problem regarding energy cooperation involves Mexico, since there is already relatively free trade in energy between the United States and Canada, as well as investment in each other's energy industries. The Mexican energy industry, in contrast, remains state-owned. Mexico's constitution gives the state control over most aspects of exploration, exploitation, refining, and pipelining of oil, gas, and petrochemicals. Some parts of the energy sector, however, have been opened to private investment, both domestic and foreign, in recent years. Given Mexico's growing energy shortages, pressure is building within the country for some kind of energy reform. The combination of needed energy reforms within Mexico and the desire for an immigration agreement with the United States may make it easier to achieve some kind of energy/immigration trade-off in the coming years.

The Impact of the Iraq War
on U.S.-Mexican Relations

The sense of shared interests between the United States and Mexico, which had weakened following the attacks of September 11, 2001, gave way altogether in light of Washington's decision to topple the Iraqi regime of Saddam Hussein. The differences between the United States and Mexico over Iraq were magnified by Mexico's membership in the UN Security Council, including its occupation of the presidency of that body in April 2003. The deteriorating relationship was also made worse by President Fox's behavior. Instead of playing down the differences between the two neighbors, he chose to use resurgent anti-Americanism in Mexico, caused by opposition to the war, to revive his flagging political support at home.

The Bush administration initially had not intended to seek the support of the UN Security Council for its decision to bring about regime change in Iraq. Ultimately, however, Secretary of State Powell persuaded President Bush to bring the issue before the Security Council in order to enhance both the legitimacy of and support for the effort to oust the Iraqi dictator. President Bush and his closest advisers apparently believed that Mexico would vote in favor of the U.S. decision, given Bush's close personal relationship with Fox and Mexico's high level of economic interdependence with the United States. Mexico, however, had never supported military action by one foreign power against another. Instead, it had consistently opted for diplomatic solutions to international conflicts, especially those involving the United States.

In fact, one of the reasons why Mexico had sought a temporary seat on the Security Council was to try to offset what it saw as Washington's tendency to resort to the unilateral use of force in the international arena. Another reason for its decision was the desire to showcase Mexico's new democracy. Much of Mexico's traditional foreign policy establishment had been unenthusiastic about the Fox administration's campaign for a Security Council seat because it feared that such a move would inevitably put Mexico on a collision course with Washington, which is exactly what happened.[16]

By the time Mexico had to vote on a UN resolution involving Iraq, Mexico had a new foreign minister. Jorge Castañeda had resigned the position in January 2003. His replacement was Luis Ernesto Derbez, an economist who Fox had initially appointed as his minister of economy. Although Derbez was considered more low-key than Castañeda, neither Mexico's public profile nor its position on the Iraq issue changed after Castañeda left the government. This indicates either that the position was shared by both the old and new foreign ministers or, more likely, that Mexico's opposition to U.S. policy toward Iraq came from the very top—that is, from President Fox himself.

Mexico did not try to conceal its initial intention to abstain on the vote on the U.S.-backed resolution concerning Iraq. When France succeeded in getting the United States to accept a more ambiguously worded resolution concerning what would happen if Saddam Hussein did not disarm, Mexico voted with France in favor of the compromise resolution. The United States subsequently introduced a second resolution supporting military action in Iraq, which it withdrew once it became clear that it would not pass. Instead of dropping the matter in the interest of limiting the damage to U.S.-Mexican relations, however, Mexico publicly announced that it would have voted against that resolution had it been brought to a vote.

The Fox administration's position on Iraq reflected Mexican public opinion, as captured in a variety of polls, and helped reverse what had been a steady decline in domestic support for his administration. It also expressed Fox's own religious values, particularly his belief that the use of force was morally wrong. However, Mexico's opposition to the United States on an issue of such high priority for Washington clearly would have negative repercussions for Fox's ability to work constructively with the U.S. administration during his and President Bush's remaining years in office.

Despite the high stakes for Mexico, there is no evidence that the Fox administration ever encouraged a public debate on the Iraq issue. Nor did it try to explain the motivations behind the Bush administration's policy toward Iraq. Mexico may have believed that any possibility of reviving the special relationship that had initially existed between the two presidents had disappeared after September 11, and therefore Mexico had little to lose by pursuing a course in opposition to Washington. It is also possible that Mexico regarded the U.S.-Mexican relationship as sufficiently mature to allow for such differences of opinion. Still another possibility is that Mexican leaders saw the United States and Mexico as so interdependent that Washington would ultimately conclude that it was in its own interest to deal with the bilateral agenda despite the differences between the two administrations. Whatever the reasons for Mexico's unnecessarily confrontational stance on the Iraq issue, however, the result was the weakening of the very special relationship between the United States and Mexico that characterized the early months of the Bush and Fox administrations. The continuing war against global terrorism will also prevent Washington from giving Mexico the attention it initially enjoyed and continues to want. Given the many political, economic, and social ties between the two countries, however, the bilateral relationship will continue to remain "special" in both good times and bad.

Conclusion

With the benefit of hindsight, the increasingly constructive and cooperative environment that characterized U.S.-Mexican relations from the late 1980s until September 11, 2001, reflected both permanent and temporary developments. Of the former, the most important was NAFTA, which strengthened the economic ties between the United States and Mexico. The key temporary development was the easing of national security concerns in the period between the end of the Cold War and the attack of September 11, which allowed Washington to shift its priorities regarding Latin America from security concerns to economic issues.

The fact that the United States experienced an economic boom during this period also contributed to improved relations between the two countries. Put simply, it is hard to be anti-U.S. when you are sharing in the prosperity of your northern neighbor.

The end of the U.S. economic boom more or less coincided with the terrorist attacks of September 11. Suddenly, the "win-win" situation that had characterized U.S.-Mexican relations disappeared. Greater economic interdependence with the United States became a mixed blessing at best for many Mexicans. And the U.S. preoccupation first with the war on terrorism and then with regime change in Iraq diverted Washington's attention from the special relationship that the new Bush administration had sought to establish with Mexico during its earliest days. Furthermore, Mexico's new democratic politics, which had initially generated considerable attention and goodwill on the part of Washington, also began to lose some of its shine. Increasingly, democracy has come to be equated with a degree of political fragmentation and stalemate that make it difficult for Mexico to pass the reforms needed to revive its sluggish economy.

Unfortunately, the relatively benign international situation of the 1990s is unlikely to return any time soon. The recent revival of economic growth in the United States, however, should help smooth over some of the rough spots in the bilateral relationship, although it will not eliminate key problems. In particular, no matter who is president of the United States in the coming years, Washington will have to give top priority to security issues and Mexico, together with its Latin American neighbors, will continue to feel neglected by the United States.

The United States, however, will never be able to ignore Mexico, given the high degree of interdependence between their economies and their people. Negotiations and cooperation will continue to be necessary in order to deal with bilateral issues such as immigration, drugs, trade, and the like. It is even possible that the United States and Mexico will reassess their behavior over the past several years and decide to adopt new approaches to both bilateral and international relations. The United States may decide it is in its interest to work more closely with multilateral institutions for the purpose of defeating terrorism and bringing peace to the Middle East, which would please Mexico. Mexico may decide that it could make a larger contribution to world peace by fighting the enemies of democratic development rather than the United States.

At this point, the only certainty is that the coming years will be challenging ones for U.S.-Mexican relations. The United States and Mexico have many common interests, but many divergent ones as well. The fact that Mexico is a new democracy further complicates bilateral relations, as does the fact that the United States is the one remaining global superpower. Yet in both cases, the benefits to the United States of having a democratic Mexico on its southern border, and the benefits to Mexico of having an economic and political powerhouse to its north, far outweigh the costs. As a result, although bilateral relations will continue to have their high and low points in future years, there is no way that the bilateral agenda can be ignored for long.

Notes

1. Stacey Wilson-Forsberg, "Canada and Mexico: Searching for Common Ground on the North American Continent," Canadian Foundation for the Americas (FOCAL), Quebec, February 2002.

2. "Old ID Card Gives New Status to Mexicans in US," *New York Times,* August 25, 2003, pp. 1, 13.

3. Robert S. Leiken, "Enchilada Lite: A Post-9/11 Mexican Migration Agreement," Center for Immigration Studies, March 2002, Washington, D.C.

4. Ginger Thompson, "After 9/11, Fox Still Waits for U.S. Moves on Mexico," *New York Times,* September 13, 2002.

5. Ibid.

6. For an excellent analysis of the NAFTA agricultural tariff issue, see Sergio Sarmiento, "NAFTA and Mexico's Agriculture," *Hemisphere Focus* 11, no. 7, Center for Strategic and International Studies (CSIS), Washington, D.C., March 4, 2003.

7. "Who Goes There?" *The Economist,* January 17, 2002.

8. "Let Us Be Your Frontier Post," *The Economist,* October 11, 2001.

9. Ibid.

10. Ibid.

11. Robert S. Leiken, "An Immigration Bargain," *Boston Globe,* March 22, 2002.

12. Leiken, "Enchilada Lite," p. 10.

13. "Let Us Be Your Frontier Post," *The Economist,* October 11, 2001.

14. Robert S. Leiken, "Immigration Accord Would Help Mexico Lock Our 'Back Door,'" *Arizona Republic,* March 18, 2002.

15. Stacey Wilson-Forsberg, "North American Integration: Back to the Basics," Canadian Foundation for the Americas (FOCAL), Quebec, August 2002, p. 8.

16. Luis Rubio, "The Vote that Wasn't," *Hemisphere Focus* 11, no. 8, Center for Strategic and International Studies (CSIS), Washington D.C., March 4, 2003.

Acronyms and Abbreviations

AFL-CIO	American Federation of Labor—Congress of Industrial Organizations
APEC	Asia Pacific Economic Cooperation
CFE	Federal Electricity Commission
CIDAC	Research Center for Development
CIDE	Center for Research and Teaching in Economics
EPR	Popular Revolutionary Army
FARC	Colombian Armed Revolutionary Forces
GATT	General Agreement on Tariffs and Trade
GDP	gross domestic product
ICC	International Criminal Court
IDEA	International Institute for Democracy and Electoral Assistance
IFE	Federal Electoral Institute
IMSS	Mexican Institute for Social Security
INEGI	National Institute of Statistics, Geography and Computer Sciences
INS	Immigration and Naturalization Services
ISSSTE	Institute of Social Security for State Workers
kWh	kilowatt hours
NADB	North American Development Bank
NAFTA	North American Free Trade Agreement
NGO	nongovernmental organization
OAS	Organization of American States
OECD	Organization for Economic Cooperation and Development
Oportunidades	renamed and expanded Ministry of Social Development

PAN	National Action Party
PEMEX	Petróleos Mexicanos (Mexican Petroleum)
PISA	Program for International Student Assessment
PNR	National Revolutionary Party
PPP	Plan Puebla Panama
PRD	Democratic Revolutionary Party
PRI	Institutional Revolutionary Party
PRM	Party of the Mexican Revolution (now the PRI)
Progresa	Food, Health, and Education Program
Pronasol	National Solidarity Program
Sedesol	Ministry of Social Development
SEP	Ministry of Public Education
SNTE	National Union of Educational Workers
Telmex	Mexican Telephone Company
TPA	Trade Promotion Authority
UN	United Nations
UNESCO	United Nations Educational, Scientific, and Cultural Organization
VAT	value-added tax

Selected Bibliography

Bosworth, Barry P., Susan M. Collins, and Nora Claudia Lustig, eds. *Coming Together?: Mexico–United States Relations.* Washington, DC: Brookings Institution Press, 1997.

Camp, Roderic Ai. *Mexico's Mandarins: Crafting a Power Elite for the 21st Century.* Berkeley: University of California Press, 2002.

———. *Politics in Mexico: The Democratic Transformation.* New York: Oxford University Press, 2002.

Campos, Julieta. *Qué Hacemos con los Pobres.* Mexico City: Alfaguara, 1995.

Castañeda, Jorge G. "Los ejes de la política exterior de México," *Nexos* 22, no. 288 (December 2001).

Davidow, Jeffrey. "Estados Unidos–México: La responsabilidad compartida," *Nexos* 23, no. 288 (December 2001).

Dominguez, Jorge, and Alejandro Poiré. *Towards Mexico's Democratization: Parties, Campaigns, Elections and Public Opinion.* New York: Routledge, 1999.

González, Guadalupe. "Foreign Politics Strategies in a Globalized World: The Case of Mexico," in Joseph Tulchin and Ralph H. Espach (eds.), *Latin America in the New International System.* Boulder, CO: Lynne Rienner Publishers, 2001.

Grayson, George. *Mexico: Corporatism to Pluralism.* New York: Harcourt-Brace, 1997.

Heath, Jonathan. *Mexico and the Sexenio Curse: Presidential Successions and Economic Crises in Modern Mexico.* Washington, DC: Center for Strategic and International Studies, 1999.

Krauze, Enrique. *Biography of Power—A History of Modern Mexico 1818–1996.* New York: HarperCollins Publishers, 1997.

Levy, Daniel C., et al. *Mexico: The Struggle for Democratic Development.* Los Angeles University of California Press, 2001.

Lustig, Nora. *The Remaking of an Economy.* Washington, DC: Brookings Institution Press, 1992.

Pastor, Robert A. *Toward a North American Community: Lessons from the Old World for the New.* Washington, DC: Institute for International Economics, 2001.

Purcell, Susan Kaufman, and Luis Rubio, eds. *Mexico Under Zedillo.* Boulder, CO: Lynne Rienner Publishers, 1998.

Roett, Riordan, ed. *Mexico's Private Sector: Recent History, Future Challenges.* Boulder, CO: Lynne Rienner Publishers, 1998.

———. *The Challenge of Institutional Reform in Mexico.* Boulder, CO: Lynne Rienner Publishers, 1995.

Rubio, Luis. *Tres Ensayos: Fobaproa, Privatización y TLC.* Mexico City: Editorial Cal y Arena and Centro de Investigación para el Desarrollo, A.C., 1999.

Salinas de Gortari, Carlos. *Mexico: The Policy and Politics of Modernization.* Mexico City: Plaza y Janés, 2002.

Serrano, Mónica, ed. *Governing Mexico: Political Parties and Elections.* London: University of London, 1998.

Silva-Herzog Márquez, Jesús. *El Antiguo Régimen y la transición en México.* Mexico City: Planeta, 1999.

Smith, Clint E. *Inevitable Partnership: Understanding Mexico-U.S. Relations.* Boulder, CO: Lynne Rienner Publishers, 2000.

Tulchin, Joseph S., and Andrew D. Selee, eds. *Mexico's Politics and Society in Transition.* Boulder, CO: Lynne Rienner Publishers, 2003.

Ugalde, Luis Carlos, and Armand B. Peschard-Sverdup. *The Mexican Congress: Old Player, New Power.* Washington, DC: Center for Strategic and International Studies, 2000.

The Contributors

Edna Jaime has been the general director of the Centro de Investigación para el Desarrollo, A.C. (CIDAC), Mexico City, since 2002. She is currently investigating savings and the informal economy in Mexico. Jaime first joined CIDAC as an associate investigator in 1989. While at CIDAC she has published various works that explore contemporary Mexican politics, the rule of law, public policy, and economic development.

Juan Pardinas joined CIDAC as a researcher in 1999. In addition, he works as a columnist for the daily periodical *Reforma* and is currently a Ph.D. candidate at the Government Department of the London School of Economics. Before joining CIDAC, Pardinas served as an international correspondent for *CNN en Español* in both India and Japan.

Susan Kaufman Purcell is vice president of the Americas Society and the Council of the Americas in New York City. Between 1981 and 1988 she was a senior fellow and director of the Latin America Project at the Council on Foreign Relations. She was also a member of the U.S. State Department's Policy Planning Staff, with responsibility for Latin America and the Caribbean between 1980 and 1981. Dr. Purcell is a former professor of political science at the University of California, Los Angeles. She is the editor and author of numerous publications, including *Cuba: The Contours of Change, Mexico Under Zedillo,* and *Brazil Under Cardoso,* and writes a monthly column for *AméricaEconomía.*

Andrés Rozental is the founding partner of Rozental & Asociados, a political and economic consulting firm established in 1997, in Mexico City. Concurrently, he has been president of the Mexican Council on Foreign Relations since January 2002. Prior to this, Rozental was ambassador at large and special presidential envoy for President Vicente Fox during the first year of his administration. Previously, he was Mexico's ambassador to the United Kingdom from 1995 to 1997 and to Sweden between 1983 and 1988. Rozental also served as deputy minister of foreign affairs of Mexico from 1988 to 1994.

Luis Rubio has been the president of CIDAC since 2002. Prior to becoming president he served as the general director since 1991. Previously, he was an adviser to Mexico's secretary of the treasury from 1980 to 1981, and worked at Citibank in Mexico from 1979 to 1981. Dr. Rubio is a member of the board of directors of Banamex, the Human Rights Commission of Mexico City, and the Mexico Equity and Income Fund.

Luis Carlos Ugalde is the president of the general council of Mexico's Federal Electoral Institute (IFE). Ugalde has taught classes at the ITAM in Mexico, as well as at Georgetown University and the American University in Washington, D.C. His areas of research include: the Mexican Congress and the oversight of public spending, executive-legislative relations, transparency and payments, and the causes and impact of institutional corruption. He has also published two books in both English and Spanish.

Index

About the Book

Mexico made a peaceful transition to democracy when it elected opposition candidate Vicente Fox president in July 2000—an event that has had a profound impact on the country's political system, its economic and social policy, and its international relationships. *Mexico Under Fox* examines the elements of continuity and change found in Mexico today.

The authors consider the changing nature of Mexico's party system and the growing influence of noninstitutional political actors. They also explore the debate over social-policy reform and the conflict between vested economic interests and the forces favoring a more open economy. In the final chapters, they discuss the impact of Mexico's democratic transition, as well as the September 11 terrorist attacks, on Mexico-U.S. relations.

Luis Rubio is president of CIDAC (Center of Research for Development), an independent research institute in Mexico. His numerous publications include *Mexico's Dilemma: The Political Origins of Economic Crisis*. **Susan Kaufman Purcell** is vice president of the Americas Society and the Council of the Americas. Dr. Purcell is coeditor, with Luis Rubio, of *Mexico Under Zedillo*.